AF488391

I AM MASTERPIECE

Embracing Your Journey as God's Work of Art

DERRICK SERIANNI

Copyright © 2024 | I AM MASTERPIECE LLC

All rights reserved. Reproduction, distribution, or transmission of any part of this publication in any form or by any means, including photocopying, recording, or other electronic or mechanical methods, is prohibited without the prior written permission of the publisher, except for brief quotations included in critical reviews and specific non-commercial uses authorized by copyright law.

ISBN Paperback: 979-8-9913822-0-5
ISBN eBook: 979-8-9913822-1-2
ISBN Audiobook: 979-8-9913822-2-9

Published By: I AM Masterpiece LLC
10580 N McCarran Blvd.
STE 588, Reno, NV 89503

Book Production | Book Your Brand LLC
Editor | David Lloyd Strauss | DavidStrauss.com
Cover Design | Astonished Man Design, Inc. | Keith Alexis
AstonishedMan.com

I AM Masterpiece Series | Book One

PRAISE FOR I AM MASTERPIECE

"I couldn't be more excited to endorse these life lessons of a man I know is pursuing God like never before. I've known many men who were successful in life, business, seemingly in their faith but Derrick stands out to me as someone who is genuine in his desire to not just meet with God, but help you meet with God as well. I pray this book can be a tool that we can all use, grow with, and learn from as we join God in the work, He's doing in all of our lives each day. Thank you, Derrick, for sharing your story and your wisdom with us."

—Chris Cleveland
Lead Singer, Stars Go Dim
Franklin, Tennessee

"I was blessed to have met Derrick Serianni at an event around the time that he was finishing this book... I remember my father saying that God will get the glory out of the darkest and hardest situations, in our lives, if we will allow it. I believe "I Am Masterpiece" is Derrick allowing God to get the glory out of a dark and hard situation. I often wonder what advice the prodigal gave to his children. I Am Masterpiece is a look into the best of fatherly advice. I recommend this wonderful book and I believe that many will be able to use his suggestions and truths to live lives that honor a Holy God."

—Cliff Preston, The Band Table
Pastor, Singer, Songwriter, Entrepreneur
Smackover, Arkansas

"Derrick's journey is full of incredible highs and lows, success and struggle, faith and doubt. Where God has led him is truly miraculous and an inspiration to all. Too many Christians are living an excessive consumption diet and not funding the mission of Jesus' love for the not-yet-found and the poor. I could see Derrick totally making an impact in that space!"

—Dan Jacobsen
Pastor, Heartland Community Church
Olathe, KS

"I have known Derrick for over 10 years. He has always been a man of character and faith, and this book shares how he overcame the ultimate test of faith: facing death. His book is an excellent read for those going through any challenge. The apostle Paul shares in 2 Corinthians 1:8-10 these words: '… We were under great pressure, far beyond our ability to endure, so that we despaired of life itself. Indeed, we felt we had received the sentence of death. But this happened that we might not rely on ourselves but on God, who raises the dead. He has delivered us from such a deadly peril, and he will deliver us again. On him we have set our hope that he will continue to deliver us…' Derrick knows these verses firsthand. This book will change thousands of lives. You will definitely enjoy it!"

—Bob Goshen
Author, Speaker, & Mentor
Montgomery, Texas

"I had the privilege of being one of the first people to read Derrick's book. Derrick has a powerful testimony that will inspire you and give you hope. His heart to help people and see them succeed has been born through his own life experiences that bleed through every page. His clear and simple communication will inspire and help many people who are stuck in patterns of self/destructive behavior. I'm certain that as you read this book you will be blessed and encouraged."

—Michael Servello
Senior Pastor Redeemer Church
Utica, New York

"I have known Derrick for over ten years. When I first met him, I was drawn to his entrepreneurial spirit and his energy and excitement for life. Having spent time with him I know him as an overcomer. And now he has overcome this life-threatening health issue which has given him even greater clarity and purpose in life. He is an authentic individual. He shares that and his heart in this work."

—Terry Zeitlow, Ph.D.
Higher Education Administration
Longview, Texas

"Derrick walked into my life years ago through a mutual friend. You can measure a man and his faith by the evidence that shows up in their life, fruits of the spirit to be precise. I've never seen more spiritual activity in a single life!

He has courageously walked through a near fatal heart attack, the recovery process, and still made time to help me through my own crises of faith. He has been such a blessing to me and my family and I don't have words for it, but I can tell you the first person I call to help me stop and think things through is Derrick. This book, initially written for his son, is full of wisdom and I'm now using it for me and my children. Derrick has a unique way of looking at things and it always comes back to Jesus, which is exactly where I want to be as I raise my children and walk through life."

—Gary Rees
JK Capital & Medical Consultant Owner
Huntington Beach, California

"Derrick Serianni is one of the few people I know that isn't afraid to speak about his faith in God along the way to personal development. I reached out to him during the hardest time of my life and he introduced me to I AM MASTERPIECE, a practical guide to living your best life through faith, business, and personal development. I have known Derrick over 25 years, and I know for certain his desire to help people, you can feel it in every page of his book. I AM MASTERPIECE should be something you revisit and apply daily, especially his 4D Method of approaching goals through the application of faith."

—Corey Carbon
Co-Founder & CEO of Pivotal Point Capital
Valencia, CA

"We have been blessed for many years to know Derrick. We met doing sales together over 2 decades ago and have had the pleasure of watching him grow personally and professionally. His book I AM MASTERPIECE is a beautiful crash course in life, personal and spiritual growth. This book is for any one desiring to succeed in life and business. We know this will bless anyone reading it to flourish! You will finish it feeling inspired, educated, and get a better understanding of who you are and be more aware of those around you personally and professionally."

—Nolan & Tiffany Passick
Business Owners Real Estate & Direct Sales
Berrian Springs, MI

"I AM Masterpiece" is truly a profound and timely work of art, especially in today's society where depression and anxiety are at an all-time high. Derrick writes with passion, purpose, and experience through his own journey. This book is inspiring and impactful for generations to come."

—Nick Palumbo
Author, Life and Business Coach
Katonah, New York

In Loving Memory...

These three people had a profound influence on my upbringing:

Anita Marie Deal (my grandmother),

Baptist "Uncle Bud" Serianni (my great uncle)

Daniel Thomas Serianni, Sr. (my dad).

My prayer is that all of you who read this book will have the pleasure of meeting them someday in heaven.

GRAMA DEAL & DERRICK

UNCLE BUD AND DERRICK

DERRICK WITH HIS DAD

DERRICK'S DAD

CONTENTS

Foreword … .. **15**

Prologue. … **23**

Introduction … .. **29**

From Cracked Chest to Transformation … … … … … … … … … … … .. **35**

Core Beliefs.. … .. **37**

DISCOVERY

1. Who Am I?. … .41

2. How Did I Get Like This? … … … … … … … … … … … … … … … … .. 45

3. Do We Have Gates of Entry?. … … … … … … … … … … … … … … … .51

4. What Kind of Influences Have Power? … … … … … … … … … … … 57

5. Who Is A Born Learner?. … … … … … … … … … … … … … … … … … 63

6. What Does God Have To Do With It? … … … … … … … … … … … 69

7. Who Am I Truly?. … … … … … … … … … … … … … … … … … … … 79

8. Do You Value Time?. … … … … … … … … … … … … … … … … … … .. 83

9. Do I Really Need A Coach? … … … … … … … … … … … … … … … 87

10. Why Can't I Wing It? … … … … … … … … … … … … … … … … … .91

11. Who Is Called To Lead? … … … … … … … … … … … … … … … … 95

DEFINE & DESIGN

12. How Healthy Am I? … … … … … … … … … … … … … … … … … … ..101

The Four Dimensions Of Development For Healthy Living … … .. **105**

13. What Significance Do Detailed Plans & Actions Have?.. … … … .. **129**

14. Why Wishes Don't Work. Smart Goals Do.. … … … … … … … ..**133**

Detailing Your SMART Goals Journey … … … … … … … … … … . **137**

15. Do You Have The Power To Transform Your Life? … … … … ..**143**

16. Do We Choose Our Personality? … … … … … … … … … … … … ..**151**

17. Why A Compilation of Personality Profiles Helps.. 155

18. How We View Others Matters.. 165

19. What About Judging Ourselves And Others?. 169

20. How To Understand Society In Four Categories . .. .173

DECIDE & DECLARE

21. How to Implement Revealed Information to Improve Relationships. ..181

22. Do We All Go Through Stages Of Learning? . .. .189

23. How Relating To Others Can Be Put To Use.. 193

24. How Endorsable Am I?. 203

25. Why Do Relationships Have Ultimate Value? 209

Bonus Chapter **219**

Join the Bible Study **225**

Community Invitation **227**

Afterword From My Beautiful Bride, Anneliese **229**

Acknowledgments **233**

FOREWORD

When I first met Derrick Serianni in October 2011, the word "persistence" jumped right out. Derrick wrote many emails to me, explaining how God used my story to get his attention. I remember Derrick explaining that even though he had gone through many ups and downs in his journey through life, he had this empty feeling inside that he was always trying to fill, and no amount of money, women, or success would satisfy it.

Derrick made it clear he was heartbroken, and no matter what he put his hands on, it didn't seem to work. He was about to make a horrible decision to sell drugs to make up for the money he lost gambling. But after hearing my story and committing his life to God, Derrick decided NOT to go through with the drug deal and chose to follow a path paved by Jesus instead.

I have to admit, it is quite humbling to see how God used my story to impact him. Derrick has thanked me several times for having the courage to tell my story. I continually remind him that it was Jesus who got his attention, and now I'm thrilled to see Derrick use his life experiences to serve the people God puts around him.

Over the past 12 years, I have seen him persevere through life's challenges while remaining steadfast in his relationship with God and continually looking for ways to better himself and his family. Speaking of his family, I know firsthand his commitment to his wife, Anneliese, and his son, Danny. Derrick always wants to lead his family from the front and is never afraid of a challenge. When you first spend time with Derrick, you might say to yourself, "Man, he is quiet." Please don't assume anything negative; he is always assessing the situation so he can take the best course of action to serve the people around him. I have seen him speak on stage on more than one occasion and have been telling him for years to do more of it.

After his heart attack in December 2022, he spent well over a year writing this book. I AM MASTERPIECE is more than just a book; it's a gateway of thoughts, beliefs, and actions that turn into an incredible curriculum for personal, professional, and spiritual development. I can see clearly how he can use his God-given gifts to inspire people from all walks of life to live better lives.

He is keenly qualified to lead people in the areas he describes in this book, not to mention the many relationships he has cultivated over the years, which he could introduce you to. Derrick gets true fulfillment from seeing others overcome their challenges and succeed.

As you read, I AM MASTERPIECE, you will find it a testament to the power of recognizing your worth through the lens of our Creator, specifically focusing on how Jesus sees us. Derrick invites readers on a journey of self-discovery, grounded in the understanding that your true value and purpose are defined not by the world's standards but by your relationship with God.

Through its pages, I AM MASTERPIECE emphasizes the idea that we are intricately designed by God, each of us a unique work of art—a MASTERPIECE in the eyes of Jesus. It's a call to action to embrace our God-given identity, to see ourselves as He sees us— fearfully and wonderfully made.

This is an offer you don't want to refuse.

Be Blessed,

Michael Franzese

Bestselling Author & Speaker

At one time a caporegime (captain) in the Italian mafia and in Fortune Magazine's Top 50 Wealthiest Mob Bosses. He went from prison to a brave new life following Jesus. No one is so bad that they can't be forgiven.

MICHAEL · DERRICK · ANNELIESE · DANNY

TO MY SON...

Dear Danny,

As you grow and find your path in life, I want to share something deeply important with you—a kind of legacy that transcends the usual bounds of inheritance. It isn't comprised of material wealth or tangible assets, but rather, it embodies a treasure trove of wisdom and spiritual insights that I have gathered throughout my journey in life.

Within the pages of I AM MASTERPIECE, I have poured the essence of what I've learned, not just through personal experiences but also through the profound teachings of our Christian faith. This book is more than just a collection of thoughts; it is a manual designed to guide you, offer comfort, and challenge you to grow in faith and character.

Each chapter and word are carefully chosen to help you navigate the complexities of life with a steadfast spirit. From understanding who you are in God's eyes to recognizing the value of time and relationships, this book aims to equip you with everything you need to live a life that is both fulfilling and pleasing to God.

Consider this book your spiritual inheritance, something to turn to when the road gets tough, when you're in need of guidance, or when you want to feel a connection to the lessons, I am passing on to you. It is my deepest prayer that these insights will serve as a beacon for you, illuminating your path as you make your way in the world.

Take these words to heart, and remember that you are indeed a MASTERPIECE, crafted by God's hand, destined for great things if you choose to walk in His ways.

I am incredibly proud of the man you are becoming, and I am here, always, to support you along the way.

With all my love and blessings,

Dad

DERRICK AND DANNY

PROLOGUE

In the middle of a near-death experience, all my thoughts immediately went to my son Danny, my wife Anneliese, and pleading with God about all the things I still wanted to do.

I originally wrote this manuscript for my son as a manual of sorts that Danny could thumb through on his nightstand at his leisure, containing the lessons I've learned on my journey through life. I wanted to ensure that when I left this world, he would have something to guide him and point him to the timeless lessons I thought were imperative for him to take note of. The manual would have to include personal and professional development, the importance of relationships, and the reality that Jesus exists and is alive today.

As I began to write, recovering in a recliner, inspiration often came to me through music. It definitely had, and still has, a healing effect on me. I would often pray for God to heal me quickly! It never seems fast enough, especially when it hurts even to breathe. I'm sure you can imagine.

A song was playing on my phone as I lay there, and as I listened, it felt as if God were singing to me. I know that sounds odd, but it's true. I had to play it on something through which I could really hear it. So, I connected the Bluetooth from my phone to a speaker with robust volume and bass. As the song started to play again, I got chills from my head to my toes. I felt at peace but also experienced a clear level of awareness, excitement, and fulfillment in my spirit. It's hard to explain except to tell you that I said, "OK, God, I'm listening."

Here are the truncated lyrics:

Heartbreaks a bittersweet sound
Know it well
It's ringing in my ears
And I can't understand
Why I'm not fixed by now
Begged and I pleaded
Take this pain but I'm still bleeding

Heart trusts you for certain
Head says it's not working
I'm stuck here still hurting
But you tell me

You're making a MASTERPIECE
You're shaping the soul in me
You're moving where I can't see
And all I am is in your hands
You're taking me all apart
Like it was your plan from the start
To finish your work of art for all to see you're making a MASTER-
PIECE

Guess I'm your canvas
Beautiful black and blue
Painted in mercy's hue
I don't see past this
But you see me now
Who I'll be then
There at the end
Standing there as

Your MASTERPIECE

Even though I'm hurting
I'll let you keep working
You're making a MASTERPIECE
You're shaping the soul in me

You're moving where I can't see
And all I am is in your hands...

I'll Be Your MASTERPIECE

> *MASTERPIECE – Sung by Danny Gokey*
> *From the Album "Rise" (Released in 2017)*
> *Songwriters: Bernie Herms / Emily Weisband*

ANNELIESE · DANNY · DANNY GOKEY · DERRICK

In 2017 we had a chance to meet but never thought
in 2023 God would use one of your songs to change my life,

I was so inspired by the song that I immediately said, "That's it! God, you are making a MASTERPIECE." Over the next month, as I was healing, I kept drawing, writing, praying, and thinking of ideas to express how God spoke to me. As I doodled, I AM MASTERPIECE was revealed.

"I AM" is the term God told Moses to use to describe Himself to the people of Israel in Exodus 3:14 (NLT). God also describes Himself as YHWH (Yahweh) in Exodus 3:15. I mention this because of the profound explanation of YHWH I read by Chris Lacy. Here it is:

> *"There was a moment when Moses had the nerve to ask God what His name was. God was gracious enough to answer, and the name He gave in the original Hebrew was "YHWH." Over time we've added an "a" and an "e" to get Yahweh because we prefer vowels.*
>
> *Scholars and rabbis say the letters "YHWH" represent breathing sounds or aspirated consonants. When pronounced without vowels, it sounds like breathing: YH (inhale), WH (exhale).*
>
> *A baby's first cry, their first breath, speaks the name of God. A deep sigh, groan, or gasp calls His name, too heavy for mere words. Even atheists speak His name, unaware that the breath in their lungs acknowledges God. Likewise, a person leaves this earth with their last breath when God's name no longer fills their lungs.*
>
> *When we can't utter anything else, is our cry calling out His name? Being alive means, we speak His name often. Is it heard the loudest when we're the quietest?*
>
> *In sadness, we breathe heavy sighs. In joy, our lungs feel like they will burst. In fear, we hold our breath and must breathe slowly to help us calm down. When we're about to do something hard, we take a deep breath to find our courage.*
>
> *Even in the most challenging moments, breathing gives Him praise! This universal truth is beautiful and should fill us up. God chose to give Himself a name that we can't help but speak every moment we're alive."*
>
> —*Chris Lacy: Independent Music Journalist. Author. Speaker. Leader. Teacher. (As seen on numerous blogs.)*

So, "I AM," or YHWH is inside you and always part of His MASTERPIECE. As God's children, we are all a MASTERPIECE under construction from our creation in the womb until our day of final rest.

"MASTERPIECE" is from Ephesians 2:10 (NLT):

> *"For we are God's MASTERPIECE. He has created us anew in Christ Jesus, so we can do the good things he planned for us long ago."*

Greg Laurie explains it well in an excerpt from his cornerstone note section of the NLT Bible...

> *"...You may have searched for purpose and meaning in life but found nothing satisfying. As a believer, however, you are "God's MASTER-PIECE," which means that His Spirit is working in your life to make you more like Christ and to give you a purpose for living. This verse describes part of the purpose God has for your life as His child – to do good works by helping others... The next time you see a neighbor in trouble, hear about a friend struggling with a problem, notice a coworker in distress, or see a stranger who genuinely needs a helping hand – take hold of this opportunity God has placed in your path."*

After consuming these profound truths and digesting their meaning and message, I realized that this manual, intended for my son, could help so many people, and a book was born.

INTRODUCTION

"I Just Need Some Help"

It's 9:30 PM on a Friday night. I'm in bed, struggling to stay asleep, and I can't get comfortable. After sleeping for only an hour and a half, I woke up with an extremely bad ache in my back, next to the inside of my shoulder blade. Everything hurts in the upper part of my body. My wife is downstairs on the couch with the dogs, watching TV.

So, I proceed to walk around the bedroom, asking God to take the pain away. My first instinct is to take a shower, then go to the bathroom—anything to make the pain go away. Nothing seemed to work, and as I was praying and asking myself what to do, a simple but clear thought popped into my head: *Go to the hospital now!*

I put on my sweats and started walking down the stairs. The pain worsened, and my wife walked into the kitchen.

She said, "Hey babe, what are you doing up?"

I said, "We have to go to the hospital right now."

She looked at me and said, "Now?"

I said, "Right now."

She said, "LET'S GO!"

As she was grabbing the dogs, she asked me, "Are you alright?" All I could think to say was, "I just need some help."

We got in the car, and I started to shake uncontrollably from my head to my toes.

My wife said, "It's going to be okay, babe."

I said again, "I just need some help."

She pulled out of the driveway like Mario Andretti, flashing her lights, calling 911, and passing cars over the double yellow lines on her way to the hospital. She was connected to the emergency room by 911. I was still shaking, saying repeatedly, "I just need some help." Within 10 minutes, we arrived at the emergency room, and my wife got me through the doors and got immediate attention from the doctors.

Several tests began to be administered; morphine was injected to relieve the pain, and throughout that evening and into the next morning, all the tests revealed possible issues with my heart. The doctors suggested an angiogram, which I agreed to without hesitation. After the test and being rolled into the waiting room for the results from the doctor, my wife and I were together, waiting for some concrete answers.

The cardiologist came in and said, "We found everything; no need to worry, and you are a strong man."

"Phew, okay, that sounds good," I said to Anneliese.

She smiled and said, "Thank God."

Then the doctor said, "You did have some blockages in your heart that we identified during the angiogram. I am going to draw a heart on this whiteboard so you can understand what I am saying."

He drew the heart, along with some lines representing veins. Then he said, "Every place I put an X is where you have a 75%- 95% blockage." After five Xs, I looked at Anneliese, and she looked at me, and we were both shocked.

The cardiologist continued, and when he completed his drawing, there were 10 X's! Anneliese asked, "What about the main vein they call the widow maker? How's that one?"

DOCTOR'S SKETCH OF HEART BLOCKAGES

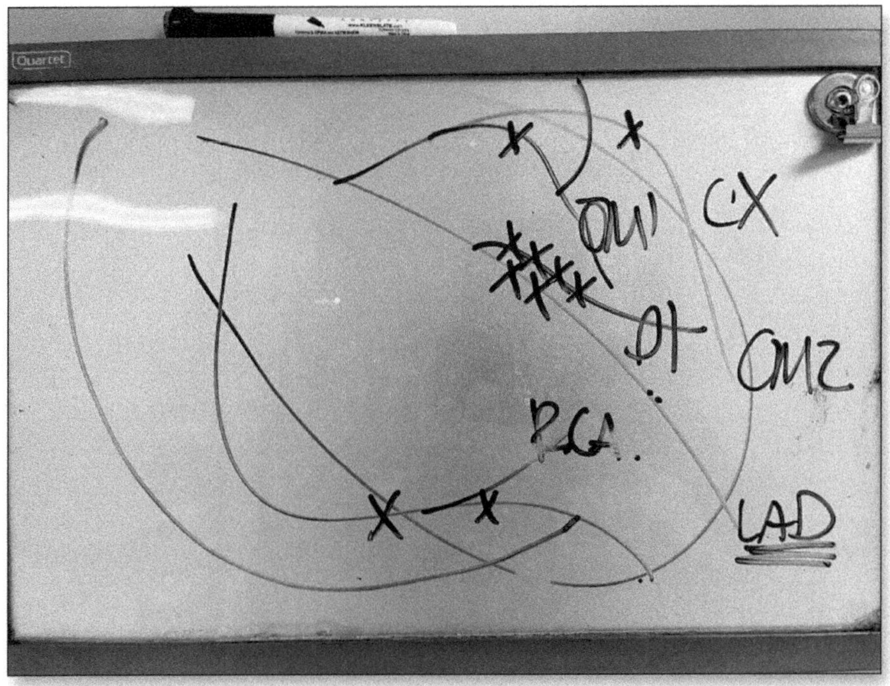

The doctor replied, "Over 95% blocked," and he said he was so happy we made it to the hospital because there was a good chance that any day after this, I could have died. Now, my wife and I were in shock and numb.

The doctor then explained that I didn't have high cholesterol or diabetes and that it must be hereditary. He also asked me a hundred times if I was a smoker, to which I replied, "No." The cardiologist then said that since I was so strong and only 49, he decided not to put any stents in during the angiogram and that the best course of action was to have open-heart surgery while simultaneously taking veins out of my legs to be grafted in for the bypass.

Now I'm thinking, holy crap! I looked at my wife and said, "Well, I guess we can think about it, right?"

She looked at me, and we both said, "Wow, these are our choices?!"

The doctor chimed in and said, "Take your time because you are not leaving here until we get this done."

Now, all I could think was that *this was serious*, and I immediately worried about my wife and son, Danny. I didn't want to leave them if something went wrong. Internally, I just started praying.

INTENSIVE CARE RECOVERY

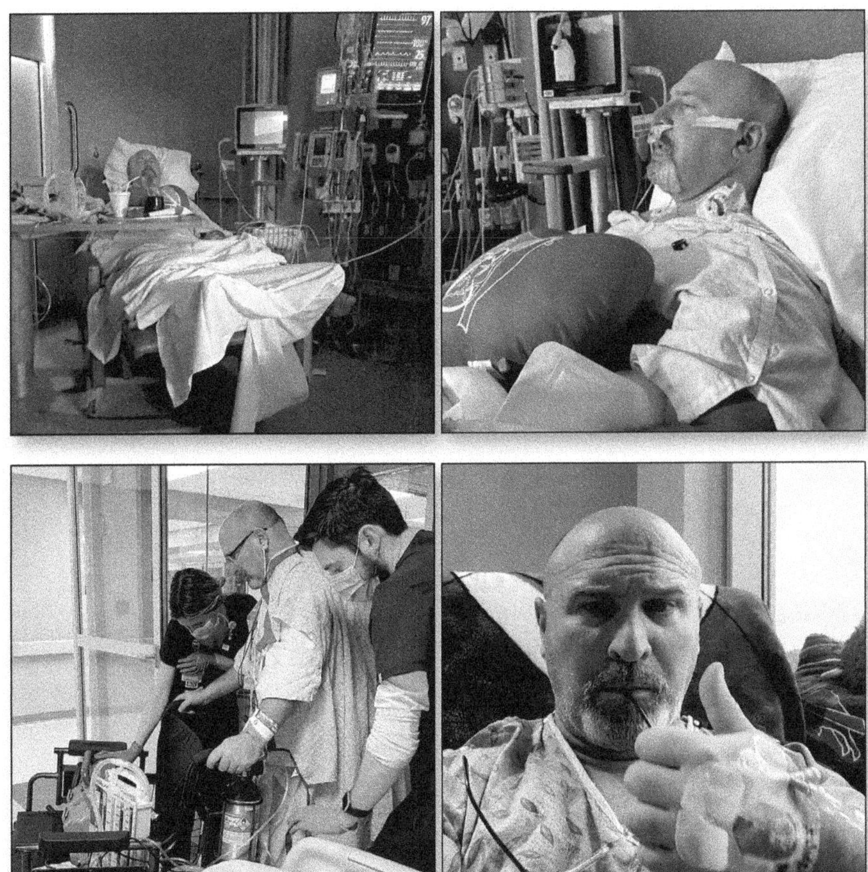

O Lord my God, I cried to you for help,
and you restored my health.
You brought me up from the grave,[a] O Lord.
You kept me from falling into the pit of death.
Psalm 30:2-3 (NLT)

FROM CRACKED CHEST TO TRANSFORMATION

Have you ever been in a similar situation of desperation, feeling lost or cornered in a moment of crisis, and wondering what to do next? When life unexpectedly falls apart, it is all too easy to fall victim to circumstances, not realizing that a moment of crisis could actually be your greatest opportunity for growth and clarity.

My moment came unexpectedly through that massive heart attack, which necessitated a quadruple bypass surgery. It was a terrifying ordeal, with my chest laid open and veins from my legs grafted to keep my heart beating. Yet, this physical and emotional trial became a profound spiritual awakening, drawing me closer to God and crystallizing my life's mission and purpose: to glorify God in everything I do.

Embarking on a Journey of Discovery

This book invites you on a transformative journey—a journey that explores the depths of personal identity and purpose and aligns them with divine intention. Through my story and the lessons learned, we will navigate the challenges and triumphs of aligning our lives with God's purpose.

1. **Part I | Discovery**: We begin by peeling back the layers of who we think we are, asking the fundamental questions that lead to a deeper understanding of our true selves and our relationship with God. It's about uncovering the essence of our being and the divine purpose behind our existence.

2. **Part II | Define & Design**: With newfound insights into our spiritual and personal identity, we move towards intentional living. This section focuses on crafting a life that reflects our beliefs and goals—personally, professionally, and spiritually—while highlighting the importance of relationships, strategic planning, and self-reflection.

3. **Part III | Decide & Declare**: The journey culminates in action. It's about making decisions that resonate with our spiritual convictions and declaring our dedication to living a life driven by purpose. This final section offers practical advice on implementing the insights gained through our journey and living out our faith in tangible ways.

A Call to Transformation

This book is born from a place of vulnerability and a profound encounter with God at the edge of life and death. It's written for anyone navigating life's uncertainties, seeking to deepen their faith, or discovering a more meaningful existence. It stands as a testament to the power of facing our mortality and finding our purpose through faith.

Whether you're looking for answers, healing, or a deeper connection with God, the words on these pages offer guidance, hope, and a pathway to a life of greater purpose and fulfillment. Let's walk this journey together—discovering, defining, and declaring our place in God's grand design.

Our journey begins with a look at the core beliefs that are the foundation of this book and then one simple question: WHO AM I?

CORE BELIEFS

Keep these in the back of your mind as you read this book.

Before we dive into our journey of "Who Am I?" let's pause and reflect on the core beliefs that will guide us forward. These five pillars are not just concepts; they are the compass by which we navigate our transformation. From grounding our actions in faith to valuing courageous leadership and fostering open dialogue, each belief lays a foundation for not just surviving but thriving in all areas of life. Keep these principles in mind as we move through each chapter, allowing them to shape our path toward a life driven by purpose. Now, let's explore these core beliefs and see how they can illuminate our journey.

1. **Faith in Jesus** is the core component that allows us to endure and thrive in business and everyday life.

2. We all can develop the **principles of strong relationships,** whether we are employees, employers, or self-employed.

3. **Courageous leaders** are those who resolve to step out from the crowd every day and should be respected and celebrated for serving their communities through word, action, or performance.

4. **Promoting Unity in Christ.** When society focuses on hope, peace, love, and joy, these attributes allow us to dig deeper, explore possibilities, and learn what the truth really is that we are all searching for.

5. Christ's followers should be **eager to communicate** with the people around them. Dialogue is imperative to productive learning and critical to understanding how to build a bridge with the

people we encounter. It also provides areas of conversation that allow us to grow and consider each other's points of view. Communication is the key to unity.

Now for the BIG question: Who Am I?

PART

One

DISCOVERY

We learn wisdom from failure much more than from success. We often discover what will do, by finding out what will not do; and probably he who never made a mistake never made a discovery.
—Samual Smiles

01

WHO AM I?

Are you frustrated with the direction of your life? Do you feel incomplete? Deep down, do you have more to offer but no clue how to unleash it? How about a fresh perspective? Let's discover together why you are who you are and formulate a plan to tap into the MASTERPIECE you were created to be.

Imagine you could start your life over. You're an artist with a brush or a potter with a large lump of clay. You are gifted and skilled, an expert in your field, and as the power of creative juices runs through your veins, you now begin to make—what? An athlete, an entertainer, a doctor, a business executive, a mathematician; are you a deep thinker schooled in philosophy, a deep-sea diver, or an explorer? What would you make of your life if you could start all over?

At some point in life, all of us ask those kinds of questions. They usually follow with the bigger questions: the kind of self-examination questions that consist of the "whys, whats, hows, whos, and dos."

- Why am I really here? Why do I think this way?

- Why do I feel the way I feel? Why do I act the way I act?

- Why do I look this way? What is my purpose in life?

- How do I earn a living with meaning and purpose?

- How do I navigate this journey called life?

- Who do I really want to be? Who should I be listening to?

- How do I strengthen the weak areas of my life?

- Why should I live more of a God-fearing life?

So, who are you? How did you begin? How did you get to where you are now, reading this book? Do you even like yourself?

As you process these questions, it's important to consider your past with the goal of understanding how it has impacted and influenced your current state. If anything needs to change, this understanding will certainly help you reach a greater goal.

"IF YOU COULD REDEFINE YOUR LIFE STARTING TODAY, USING THE 'ARTIST WITH A BRUSH' OR 'POTTER WITH CLAY' ANALOGY, WHAT MASTERPIECE WOULD YOU CREATE WITH YOUR LIFE, AND WHAT STEPS WOULD YOU TAKE TO START SHAPING THAT VISION?"

HOW DID I GET LIKE THIS?

The profound question of "WHO AM I?" naturally leads to another crucial thought: "How did I get like this?"

Now, let's peel back the layers of our lives and look into the echoes of our upbringing and the decisions we've made that have led us to who we are now. It's like standing at a crossroads, looking back at the paths we've taken, wondering how each turn, each decision, and every moment led us here.

Each of us was raised in one of four circumstances: nurtured, neutral, neglected, or a combination of these experiences. Here, we explore these influences, seeking clarity on the forces that have molded us and examining our potential for change. This is not just about understanding these forces; it's about leading us toward becoming the best versions of ourselves.

After reading each of these, which do you identify with most?

Nurtured

You were blessed to have been raised by loving parents who planned and prepared for you. They did their best to shape and mold your life by helping you make wise choices and decisions. Your parents weren't experts, but they used all the resources available to lead and guide you, which are still available to you today. Your parents will continue to be very much a part of your life, and if you're fortunate, they are still living.

Neutral

In this situation, you don't really recall a whole lot of your early childhood. Much of what happened in your life is gray, murky, and unclear. There are no big bright colors, no high-highs, or low-lows. You feel as though where you are in life just "happened," like water in the middle of a river that takes its natural course as the bend of the shoreline turns and twists. It never touches that shoreline; it just stays in the middle on its way to a destination, unsure of how it started and not sure how it will end.

Neglected

It's tragic and sad, but it happens all the time. Those who should have cared for you didn't, and your lack of parental direction has led you down some dark and disappointing corridors.

There has been too much pain and a lot of heartache, and your past has been so difficult that when prompted at the beginning of this book to consider the possibility of starting over, the idea resonated deeply within you. Thoughts like "I would love to" and "I need to start over" most likely came to mind.

Some of you, regardless of your painful past, wouldn't change a thing because, despite the pain and negativity of those experiences, they have undeniably shaped you, giving you a clearer sense of what you now desire in life. Yet, there remains a part of you that wishes for the opportunity to make adjustments to reshape your journey toward a more fulfilling direction.

Combination

We do know and acknowledge that in the day and time this book is being written, there is another category: your childhood could be a "combination" of one or more of the above experiences. You could have been nurtured by your mother and neglected by your father. Or, you may have grown up in a single-parent home, where your mother, striving to be both the provider and caregiver, left you feeling closer to a grandmother or aunt who provided the nurturing you needed.

During those formative early years, you were a little like wet cement; everyone you came in contact with left an impression on you. Whatever the circumstances, their impressions became imprints, shaping and defining your personality, character, and choices.

According to the Scriptures, those imprints do not have to be permanent, and each of these experiences is not a life sentence. God had a plan for you while you were still in the womb. He gifted you. Your God-given gifts are just that—God-given. But to receive those gifts, it is your choice to break free from your past limitations and step into living the truth of God's will.

First, you have to recognize real limitations versus perceived limitations. Training and education cannot produce an award-winning vocalist if you sound like a frog. If you're under 150 lbs., you won't make it as a linebacker in the NFL. Those limitations are real and understandable. Perceived limitations are those based on fear or self-judgment. Pulling up your proverbial bootstraps isn't going to change your real limitations. However, hard work and discipline go a long way when breaking free from perceived limitations and changing the course of your future.

You may have heard the slogan: "Be all you can be." It is offered in an advertisement by the United States Army. The leadership of every military team believes that the energy and effort you put forth in following rules of discipline can result in both a change of heart and a change of life. This applies to everyday life as well. Growing up in adverse surroundings or impoverished conditions certainly doesn't mean you're stuck there for life. There are a million examples of people who, in spite of their background, through their personal choices and a little moxie, transformed the way they moved forward.

Some time ago, I wanted to buy a new car. What I really needed was something that could seat six people. I wanted something fuel-efficient, sporty, with a convertible top, something low to the ground and nimble but high enough that I could see over the vehicles just in front of me. I wanted something fast, with a roof rack that could keep my surfboard on top. You get the idea.

They don't make that. You can't have a roof rack with a convertible, and you can't have something high enough to see over vehicles yet low to the ground. My point is simple: no one car can do it all. No one person is everything. You can't be tall and short, blonde and naturally brunette, or have blue eyes and brown eyes. In the same way, no one person can embody the fullness of each and every personality trait.

The Psalmist declared:

> *"For you formed my inward parts; you knitted me together in my mother's womb. I praise you, for I am fearfully and wonderfully made; wonderful are your works, my soul knows it very well"*
> *(Psalm 139:13-15 KJV).*

You are you, not everyone else. Whether you were nurtured, neutral, neglected, or a combination of the above, you are the sum total of the actions and reactions on your journey in life. Whether they've been good or bad, tragic or blessed, today, you are exactly where you need to be to take a good look at your life, discover why and how you got this far, and make any changes that will make for a better tomorrow.

You cannot change your past, but you can change the direction you take from this point forward. Start where you are with what you have. You may have heard, "Bloom Where You Are Planted." A more complete explanation is:

> *Each person should remain in the situation they were in when God called them.*
> *Were you a slave when you were called? Don't let it trouble you—although if you can gain your freedom, do so. For the one who was a slave when called to faith in the Lord is the Lord's freed person;*

similarly, the one who was free when called is Christ's slave. You were bought at a price; do not become slaves of human beings. Brothers and sisters, each person, as responsible to God, should remain in the situation they were in when God called them.
(1 Corinthians 7:20–24)

You only get one of these things called "life"; there are no returns or refunds, and there are no guarantees of a pedal-laden path, all green traffic lights, and every phone call answered. Life happens. What you do with it, you will discover, is a matter of choice.

"REFLECTING ON YOUR PAST, WHICH OF THE FOUR UPBRINGING SCENARIOS—NURTURED, NEUTRAL, NEGLECTED, OR A COMBINATION—DO YOU IDENTIFY WITH MOST, AND HOW HAS THAT SHAPED THE PERSON YOU ARE TODAY?"

DO WE HAVE GATES OF ENTRY?

Since we have just explored the forces that have shaped us, it's important to look closely at our senses—the gateways to our minds. Our senses are not just pathways for information but the very channels that can lead us toward transformation or trap us in cycles of negativity.

Let's explore how guarding these gates with intention and wisdom can drastically alter the course of our lives. It's about being mindful of what we consume, whether through what we see, hear, or experience, ensuring that our inner sanctum remains a place of growth, positivity, and alignment with God's will. Here, the focus shifts from the external influences that shaped us to our power over them, marking a bold move in our journey toward becoming the architects of our destiny.

Our senses—ears, eyes, nose, and mouth—serve as the primary gateways through which we receive and interact with the world around us, dictating our reactions and responses. They are paths of entry, places of access where we receive content, data, and specific information, stimulating the need for a response or reaction. These gateways are not just passageways for the mundane or the routine; they are the conduits through which the essence of our experience flows, shaping our perceptions, beliefs, and, ultimately, our actions.

Consider the experience of walking into a coffee shop. As you open the door, your senses are immediately engaged. The aroma of freshly brewed coffee (smell) fills the air, inviting and warm. The sound of steam hissing from the espresso machine (hearing) blends with the soft murmur of conversations and the clinking of cups. Your eyes (sight) are drawn to the array of pastries behind the glass counter, each more tempting than the last. Perhaps you decide to treat yourself to a croissant, and as you take that first buttery bite, the flavors explode in your mouth (taste), confirming that you made the right choice.

In this everyday scenario, each of your senses plays a crucial role in shaping your experience. They guide your reactions—the comfort you feel in the cozy atmosphere, the decisions you make, such as choosing to sit and enjoy your coffee rather than rushing out. This moment in the coffee shop is a simple yet powerful reminder of how our senses are gateways to the experiences that shape our perceptions, beliefs, and actions.

Just as consuming a spoiled meal can upset our physical well-being, exposure to harmful visuals and sounds can disturb our mental and emotional equilibrium. Imagine walking through a serene park, soaking in the peaceful sights and sounds, only to return home and bombard your senses with violent TV shows; the contrast starkly affects your inner calm. The images we absorb through our eyes, the sounds we tune into, and the words we consume can nourish our souls or poison our peace. It's a delicate balance, navigating through a world saturated with stimuli, learning to filter out the noise, and focusing on what truly enriches us. The art of discernment becomes crucial as we decide what to let in and what to keep out, understanding that these choices directly influence our well-being, our thoughts, and our path forward.

In my lifetime, I've seen some things I wish I hadn't. The images are still in my mind, and I must purposely choose not to recall them. The stories I've heard, I can still recall, remind me of events and experiences I truly wish I could forget. These days, we consume large amounts of stuff (junk) that enters our minds and influences how we view our lives and our world. For example, scrolling through social media can often feel like a double-edged sword; it keeps us connected yet bombards us with a relentless stream of curated realities, sensational news, and often negativity that can skew our perception of the world and ourselves.

This flood of information, much like junk food for the brain, can significantly shape our outlook on life and the world. There is an old saying about a computer being programmed: "Garbage in, garbage out." Oh, how I wish it had only been good. But what if I could use all the data in an effort to choose more wisely? I ate a bad oyster once; that was all it took! Now, I'm not really an oyster guy because I remember too well the stomach pain that followed.

Just as we learn from our experiences, like avoiding oysters after getting sick, we can apply similar caution to protect our minds, much like a castle fortifies its entrance to safeguard its treasures.

Think of an image of a grand castle surrounded by a moat of water and a large drawbridge with a single point of entry. With only one way in and heavily guarded, the opportunity for the adversary to find access to what you value and prize the most is severely weakened.

The concept of sanctions, which involves restricting access to materials that could enhance the capabilities of adversaries, also serves as an analogy for protecting our minds. Just as sanctions are intended to prevent or slow down the transfer of specific items to foreign adversaries, similarly, by controlling the type of information we allow through our senses and vigilantly monitoring these entry points, we can significantly reduce the likelihood of negative influences breaching our mental defenses.

"We should guard our hearts with all diligence because from out of them flow the issues of life." (Proverbs 4:23)

This verse suggests that whatever we allow to enter our hearts, if not examined and evaluated with wise processing, will undoubtedly be expressed in our lives and our actions in either positive or negative ways. One of the most practical ways to guard your heart is to put a "father filter" over your gates of entry.

None of us would willingly smell a foul odor; we immediately hold our nose, hoping to, in some way, block the stench. We all have earthly dads, but we also have a Heavenly Father. His Spirit is ready to intervene and block whatever would harm or influence you adversely. My earthly dad departed several years ago; he's in heaven now, but I can still hear his voice. When I'm face to face with an important decision, my earthly dad's wisdom still speaks. Those morsels of truth come back clearly.

Your Heavenly Father also has a speaking voice. As you become more familiar with His word, you will hear His voice saying, "Take this path, go this direction, it's time to move forward." That's the "father filter." When we slow our hurried pace and allow the Holy Spirit to speak, He will filter what is best, what is good, and what is better so that you can access a more positive and productive way of thinking.

WHEN YOU THINK ABOUT THE THINGS
YOU LET INTO YOUR MIND THROUGH
YOUR SENSES, WHAT KIND OF IMPACT DO
THEY USUALLY HAVE ON YOU? ARE THERE
SPECIFIC TYPES OF SHOWS, MUSIC, OR
CONVERSATIONS THAT LIFT YOU UP OR
BRING YOU DOWN?

WHAT KIND OF INFLUENCES HAVE POWER?

Reflecting on the gateways through which the world whispers to us, it's time to zoom out and see the bigger picture of what influences have power over our thoughts and attention. Remember the catchy TV tunes from childhood or the deep dive into books that shaped our thinking? As we grow, these influences morph, and now there's a whole digital universe vying for our attention.

From endless social media scrolls to binge-worthy TV series, the rhythm of the world is constantly tugging for our attention. Now, let's explore what kinds of influences have power and how they sway us—sometimes subtly, sometimes dramatically—from the paths we intend to walk. It's about recognizing the tunes we've been humming unconsciously and deciding if they truly harmonize with the music we mean to make with our lives.

Let's think of our childhood and consider how the thoughts and ideas conveyed to us by our parents, family, friends, teachers, peers, community, and environment influenced us. The encouragement from a teacher that sparked a lifelong passion for science, or the summer evenings spent playing baseball with neighborhood friends that taught us about teamwork and perseverance.

It is essential to recognize that in the times we live in, outside influences are even more profound and powerful than personal influences used to be because they follow us everywhere through smart devices and our global connections via the internet.

For starters, how about TV? You might be old enough to remember a whole host of commercial jingles that are still stuck in your head. You only have to hear a couple of notes, and you're singing the song, designed by a marketing department on Madison Avenue, branded on your brain with the hope of making you buy or like the products they sell. To this day, you have those words memorized and stored in your mind for instant recall when the memory is triggered.

What about literature? Maybe it's a classic business book you enjoyed that struck an inspirational note with you. I still enjoy going back to Napoleon Hill's *Law of Success* and anything John Maxwell has written to help me with leadership skills and the application of leadership principles. Lately, I've been devouring books written by Patrick Bet-David. Often, I've encouraged my clients to add to their own mental library. Pick an area that interests you the most and Google "the best book about"; now, get reading.

How about music? Everyone has a playlist of their favorite tunes or hits from their era. It could be classic rock, jazz, rhythm & blues, swing, or just the right mood music to create an atmosphere for relaxation or meditation.

It could be movies. There are so many to watch, including classics like *Gone with the Wind* or more recent treasures like *Saving Private Ryan, Gladiator,* and *The Patriot.* With all the streaming services, you can binge an entire series today, with endless shows, programs, documentaries, sports programming, and game shows; the list goes on.

What about the advent of computers? Before Google was on your phone, you would spend hours on your desktop surfing the web for information and general knowledge, and even before PlayStation and Xbox, a computer did most of your gaming!

Let's consider the power of influence more deeply. It's in your hand, your pocket, your purse, your passenger seat, never more than a few feet away from you. Yep! Your phone is no longer a simple telephonic communication device; it's now your link to the world. The world of news, shopping, reading, pictures, weather, alarms, contacts, banking, games, food—the list is as long as your collection of apps.

What's more powerful is that this point of contact is, of course, a "tool" loaded with powerful messaging designed to keep you connected. Connected to podcasts, subscriptions, data, and persuasive advertising, all intended to brand your brain with indelible images that stick and stay.

So now, more of your decisions are controlled by some business, speaker, product, or service that's hoping to lead you to them. The "pied piper" of this generation is being used to lead, just like the story. That's an actual adaptation of the real-life event; the Pied Piper filled with vengeance, came back to the little city and, with his magic flute, while the parents were in church, hypnotized the children of the village and led them to destruction. It's a sad but powerful illustration because, in some ways, the same thing is happening in our lives today.

In the book of James 4:4b, it reads, "Whoever wishes to be a friend of the world makes himself an enemy of God." The Britannica dictionary defines friendship in this way: "The state of enduring affection, esteem, intimacy, and trust between two people." Sadly, the world we live in flavors and favors a style of living and a worldview that, in most cases, is not friendly or accustomed to reverence toward God.

When reading Exodus 20, the list of God's Ten Commandments, you'll notice that much of what is depicted on TV and in movies, indulged in during Netflix binges, and consumed in popular romance novels involves the continual and repetitive breaking of those Ten Commandments.

This elusive bombardment of content that goes against the commandments is a powerful example of influential forces at play in our daily lives. It shows us how TV shows, movies, and books can guide our thoughts and behaviors, sometimes away from what we know or believe are right. When you laugh at a joke that mocks something sacred or find yourself rooting for a character living a life full of deceit, you're experiencing firsthand the kind of influence that has real power over our lives. It's these situations that remind us to be mindful of what we're letting into our minds.

I've often wondered why God's name and Jesus' name are used for swearing. Why not Mussolini or Hitler? And how many people do you know who, being so accustomed to hearing those words used for swearing, think it's strange that I even have an opinion? We have become so accustomed to hearing certain words used in certain ways that we don't even realize we're becoming desensitized. What used to be offensive language years ago is now common vernacular. The influence of the world has so impacted the way we behave and believe that we are not even aware that we've become so friendly to it.

As for why people use God's name in vain, it often comes down to habit or the influence of the culture around us rather than a deliberate intention to disrespect or offend. Many of us grow up hearing these expressions used casually, without fully grasping their meaning or impact. It becomes almost second nature to use them in everyday speech, sometimes without even thinking about it. It's like picking up slang or phrases from friends or media without realizing how they might affect others or what they truly mean.

There may be a subtle underlying belief, even among non-believers, in the existence of a higher power. During moments of anger, frustration, or vulnerability, it's almost instinctual to call upon something greater for support or release. So, whether consciously or not, invoking God's name in such instances might stem from a deep-seated human tendency to seek solace or express intense emotions by reaching out to a perceived source of strength beyond ourselves.

In 1940, the movie *Gone with the Wind* was released; the audience was shocked when Clark Gable, the male lead, used the word "damn" in a sentence. It was unprecedented for profanity to be included in a Hollywood production. Good people of faith wouldn't consider going to the movies to see that film, not with that kind of language.

We've certainly come a long way. Since then, societal norms have evolved significantly. Our minds have become desensitized, blurring the lines between what is considered good or bad, true or false, right or wrong. Ephesians 4:29 (NIV) offers guidance on this matter:

"Do not let any unwholesome talk come out of your mouths, but only what is helpful for building others up according to their needs, that it may benefit those who listen."

Behaving in this manner may not be very popular, but it's very powerful. Remember, everyone influences someone. You either influence them in a good way or in a bad way.

On a personal note, I do my best to live out these principles. At times, I fail, too. I'm not perfect and don't claim to be. I'm continually working on myself just like you—or you wouldn't be reading this book. Becoming aware of things in our lives that can negatively affect us is more than half the battle.

CONSIDERING THE VARIOUS WAYS IN
WHICH WE INTERACT WITH THE WORLD
THROUGH OUR SENSES, HOW CAN YOU
MORE INTENTIONALLY GUARD THESE
GATEWAYS TO ENSURE YOU ALLOW ONLY
POSITIVE INFLUENCES TO GUIDE YOU?

05

WHO IS A BORN LEARNER?

After considering how external influences shape our thoughts and actions, let's adjust our focus to a more innate aspect of ourselves: our natural tendency to learn and explore. From a young age, curiosity drives us to absorb everything around us, laying the foundation for who we become. This inherent desire to understand the world is what makes us all born learners. Now, let's dive into what it means to be naturally curious and how this curiosity shapes our journey through life.

Think back to early in your life, like between 2 and 7 years old. Do you remember how long it seemed to be between breakfast and lunch and lunch and dinner? How about when weekends were filled with excitement, and there were no deadlines and no timelines? Do you recall how the time until your next birthday or holiday seemed to stretch on forever? Have you ever wondered why that was? What were you expecting to experience? What were you looking forward to? How about the excitement or awe of all life's possibilities? Simply put, we were curious, information gatherers, like little sponges soaking up all the data being programmed and guided by influences that impact our understanding. Yes, we all are born learners.

What about the pain of missing people you loved to see? Why was that? How did they make you feel? What did they possess or display that made you say, "I want more of that"? Friends who were so important to you because of the way they made you feel. How far would you ride your bike to go to their house or walk in the snow to go to that party, or take a long road trip to attend that concert?

Do you remember how good it felt when you won at something or how powerful the frustration was when you lost? It's possible that around that same time, you began to become more competitive; the feeling of winning was so good, and the feeling of losing was so bad that you started to get more laser-focused on winning because of how good it felt. If by chance we lost more than we won, over the years of loss, with age came caution. We discovered that the price for winning came with a price tag. Yes, there would be a price to be paid to acquire important traits like **determination**, the drive to stay consistent and unyielding, **discipline**, the will to make more attempts without immediately seeing the fruit of our labor, and **focus**, freedom from the distractions that take us off course, and the power to silence the negative noise of our own unbelief that our goal is unattainable.

Since that seemed too costly for most of us, the older we got, the more we settled for less. We stopped taking the same chances; we didn't want to risk the loss of control or a sense of safety. It's because we're conditioned to fear. It may be hard to believe, but I've known some people who fear success because with success comes change, and they'd like to keep things just the way they are. For others, it's not success they fear; it's failure. However, both fears are attached to negative emotions that create a more cautious disposition. We become convinced that the next time, it just won't turn out the way we hope it will. We've become programmed to believe that it's probably best not to make that decision, but it's better not to take that next step. It's better to be safe than sorry, and the older we got, the more it became a routine.

Why does that happen? We were not originally created for all the negative emotions; fear is a byproduct of the fall, only developed after original sin entered the world. From that point forward, everyone was affected. It's clear that society, over time, starts conditioning us to play it safe and conform, and the natural result is that we think more negatively than positively. By allowing our influences to condition us this way, we became a product of that kind of thinking. Around that same time, and especially as we grew older, if we didn't know how to take responsibility for the failure when, in some cases, we were in part to blame, we started shifting the reason to somebody or something else, hoping we could feel better. Tragically, we didn't grow through the experience; we only went through it and defended our thought process.

The world shaped our worldview, a system of thinking, and the way society dictates how we should think. If we were fortunate and were positively influenced earlier in life, it's usually because our parents or our peers knew these principles and instilled them in us. But if not, we need to realize that our parents and peers did the best they could with what they knew or chose to know. Stop and consider for a moment that they were navigating this life with direction from their parents and peers, too, and the only way to break out of this is to be willing to change our thoughts.

External influences impact internal dispositions: Our influences condition us to believe or do whatever it is we believe and do; therefore, we become a byproduct of the thinking that flows from those environments. I'm sure you've heard the saying, "Birds of a feather flock together," or "One bad apple spoils the whole bunch." Well, here's another one: 1 Corinthians 15:33 NLT:

"Bad company corrupts good character."

The only thing we have complete control over as adults is our thoughts and behaviors. Blaming our shortcomings on our ancestral heritage is just an easy way out of behaving more responsibly. In some churches, the belief in generational curses suggests we are bound to repeat the failures of our fathers and mothers, suggesting that there is a sin gene passed along through our blood, but only from Adam. We sin because sin entered the world through him. Our parents are responsible for their sins; you are responsible for yours.

In fact, Jeremiah 31:29 NIV addresses this fact. We read:

"The word of the Lord came to me again, saying, 'What do you mean when you use this proverb concerning the land of Israel, saying, "The fathers have eaten sour grapes, and the children's teeth are set on edge"?'"

Another translation reads, "The parents ate green apples, and the children got a stomachache." This proverb was widely repeated as an excuse for bad behavior. The first half of the verse is very explicit: "As I live, says the Lord, you shall no longer use this proverb in Israel." God had tired of hearing excuses and blame casting, attempting to find fault with someone else for our failures.

Verse 30 continues the thought:

"But everyone shall die for his own iniquity; every man who eats the sour grapes, his teeth shall be set on edge."

As adults, we can begin to adopt a different way of thinking that can help us become the kind of leaders we are created to be. Wouldn't it be wise to learn from our mistakes? Certainly, we can learn from others' mistakes, and it's probably a lot easier. Once the fault-finding and blame-shifting stop and we truly begin to hold ourselves responsible, our thought life is free from that common and natural default.

The Psalmist prayed in Psalm 19:14 KJV, "Let the words of my mouth, and the meditation of my heart, be acceptable in thy sight, O Lord, my strength, and my Redeemer." He's asking God to help him with his thought life; he knew it was where decisions began, and he knew that if God directed his meditations and considerations, then his choices could be more divinely designed. I know that's what I want. In God's word, there is a great template we should use to filter our thoughts and lives. In Philippians 4:8-9 MSG, we read:

(8) Summing it all up, friends, I'd say you'll do best by filling your minds and meditating on things true, noble, reputable, authentic, compelling, gracious - the best, not the worst; the beautiful, not the ugly; things to praise, not things to curse.

(9) Put into practice what you learned from me, what you heard and saw and realized. Do that, and God, who makes everything work together, will work you into his most excellent harmonies.

You'd certainly agree it's a great prescription for a more worry-free, honest, and fruitful thought life, with no place for porn, lust, or lying in that list. Let's start fresh and develop the kind of character qualities God intended us to have. God is our creator; therefore, wouldn't He know the most about His creation?

CAN YOU RECALL A MOMENT FROM YOUR EARLY CHILDHOOD THAT PARTICULARLY FUELED YOUR CURIOSITY? HOW HAS THAT CURIOSITY SHAPED THE PERSON YOU'VE BECOME?

06

WHAT DOES GOD HAVE TO DO WITH IT?

As we step away from exploring our innate curiosity and the influences that shape us, let's move toward a deeper question: What does God have to do with all this? This next part of our journey dives into the contrast between our natural selves—prone to selfishness and mistakes—and the perfect love God extends to us. It's about understanding that beneath the layers of our actions and desires lies a fundamental truth: we are imperfect beings in need of divine guidance and grace. Let's explore how this understanding impacts our lives, choices, and, ultimately, our relationship with God.

The way God sees us is quite intriguing. I've got some bad news and some good news; let's start with the bad news first. No one ever had to learn or be taught to be selfish; the earliest cry from every child is "mine." It's that inherent rebellious side that will lie when caught, run when guilty, hide when shamed, and lust for the things it craves. The first time you hear a defiant "no" from your sweet little angel, you realize it is in us, all of us. The Bible puts it this way:

> *"For all have sinned and fall short of the glory of God."*
> *(Romans 3:23 NKJV)*

Speaking of sin, let's not forget the sinful nature we have. It's standard equipment, not an option you have to pay for or a request you have to make; every human body comes out of the womb from the manufacturer with a sinful nature. Without understanding the reason for the unending battle within us, it will always be more difficult to make the changes we hope to see in our lives unless we're aware of this normal, natural spiritual malady—a condition that affects and impacts all our choices and decisions.

What is sin? The word "sin" is an ancient archery term that means "missing the mark." This definition of sin is helpful because it brings clarity to sin's nature. When we use the two-word phrase "sin nature," it describes the natural inclination to resist or rebel, choosing to do our will rather than God's. You can miss the mark by a little, or you can miss it by a lot; however, a miss is still a miss, so sin is still a sin. One of the problems we face today is that most of us no longer agree on what the target is. For example, some people believe pleasure is the target for them; anything that hinders pleasure is a sin, even if they don't use that word. Certainly, not all pleasurable things are sinful; they just assume that.

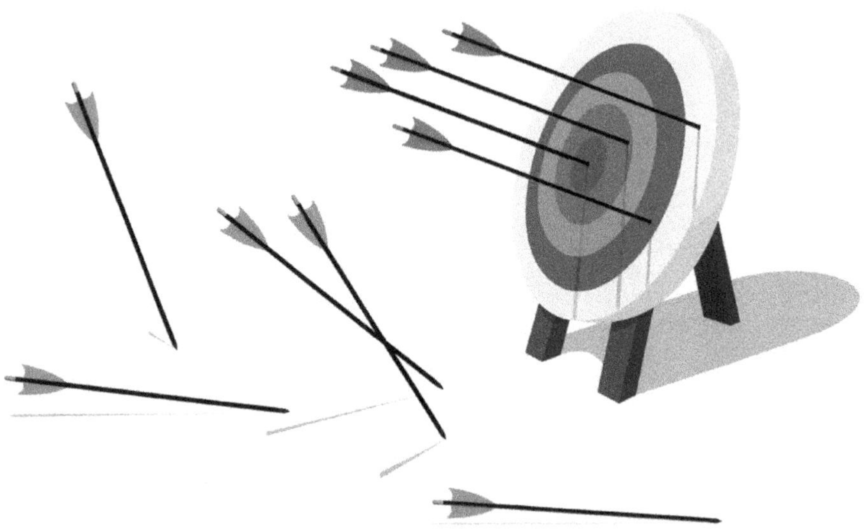

We never hit the target 100% of the time.
Misses are part of being human.

For others, the target is freedom; for them, anything that limits their or anyone else's freedom is a sin. Again, this is another erroneous assumption. God told us through His word that we're made in His image. God calls us to aim at the high calling of Christ Jesus. When we hit that target, we receive true fulfillment, which brings everlasting pleasure and peace. To be perfect, all we must do is hit the mark 100% of the time. Do I hear laughter in the room? Exactly! Nobody hits the mark 100% of the time; that's why we need a Savior.

While we're on the subject of perfection, every reader should be aware of an often-overlooked fact: there are sins of commission and sins of omission. James 4:17 (NIV) declares, "Therefore, to him who knows the good to do and doesn't do it, to him it is sin." So, whoever knows the right thing to do and fails to do it, for him, that is a sin. Sins of commission are the kind of sins that are clearly defined by commandments and warnings in God's word.

Sins of omission are the kinds of sins that are committed by simply not doing what we know in our hearts we should be doing. Your anger over a bad driver, your envy over somebody winning the mega millions, the coveting you do when looking a second time at somebody's tricked-out classic car. Need I say more? Everyone is a sinner. We all know the saying "practice makes perfect"; the more we practice something, the better we get at it. I know some people who have turned sinning into an art form. There are good grooves and rotten ruts.

Have you ever felt a sort of "rush" after performing a good deed? That sensation is known as "helper's high," and it's produced when your brain releases endorphins, the feel-good chemicals of the brain. When you do something good for someone else, your brain's pleasure centers light up, releasing endorphins and producing a high. That's a good groove.

As I mentioned, there are also rotten ruts; some bad behaviors also produce chemicals, and repeating those acts can lead to a routine of bad behavior, becoming an addiction that is now hard to break.

The good news is that Christ came into the world to save us from our sins, the horrible habits, the addictive behavior, and the pain that follows so that we could live a more productive, fruitful, and victorious life. In John 10:10 (NLT), Jesus stated, "My purpose is to give them a rich and satisfying life."

When we talk in terms of sin and behavior, I want to emphasize God's character; He is relational and transformational, so much less than transactional, where we exchange goods for services or, in our case, obedience for blessings. We've all heard from those outside faith circles that the Bible is "just a bunch of rules."

The Psalmist wrote in Psalm 119:105, "Your word is a lamp for my feet, a light on my path." The first time I read that verse, I was curious. I wanted to understand the difference between a lamp and a light. The lamp is for my feet, and the light is for my path. In the original language, the word lamp refers to a small light, in our time, like a flashlight that you'd shine while you're walking. The word for light in the text is different; it describes a bright light, an illumination.

In my imagination, I now see that with His word, I can take small daily steps with my flashlight. As I continue on that path, I discover the sunlight ahead of me, leading me to the place He has divinely designed for my journey.

Now, that certainly sounds like a friendship-type relationship. I envision walking hand in hand, or the way a good father would put his arm around his son or daughter, leading them on a more perfect path. Rather than looking at God's directives as rules, see them instead as guidelines and ground rules. Just like a guardrail on a mountain road, it's properly placed to protect and keep your loved ones safe in the family van. I find it more comforting than restrictive driving on a lonely, winding road late at night. I can have peace staying in my lane. Staying in my lane is something I choose to do; it's something I want to do; it's not something I have to do.

In the same way, if you are a Christian, you recognize God's word has been given to those who want to follow, not those who have to follow. It becomes a "love" thing! Do you remember when you first fell in love? The feelings of excitement and adventure you cherished spending time together, whether it was just holding hands, talking, or walking in the park—there didn't even need to be a park. During that time, the world seemed to stop, and your focus and devotion were 100%. If you had been asked to do anything for your love, you would not have hesitated or procrastinated. Jump? How high? How much will you spend if you have it? It really didn't matter. You were in love. It's the same way in your relationship with God if it's truly a "love" thing.

I've heard countless stories of great proposals, guys who have proposed to display their love to their future bride with grand gestures, sometimes costly and extravagant. I know a man who rented a banner that flew behind a biplane up and down the Miami coastline, with his future wife's name and the words "Will you marry me?" I know another fellow who took his future wife scuba diving; he had hidden the ring inside a shell; it was risky, and she certainly was surprised. One more, I know a man who asked the chef at a fancy restaurant to bake the ring into the dessert cake, and at the end of the meal, she got a fork full of cake and a diamond promise.

The best of all is the proposal Christ made to us on the cross with open arms, the blood of forgiveness flowing, with a promise to take us to heaven and dwell there for all eternity. Now, that's a "love thing." That truth is in place even apart from the fact that we don't deserve heaven. No one ever earned heaven; you can't. You see, the only requirement to get into heaven is sinless perfection. And no one apart from Jesus Christ ever accomplished that act of righteousness. It's been referred to as the "great exchange."

In 2 Corinthians 5:21 (TLB), we read, 'For God took the sinless Christ and poured into him our sins. Then, in exchange, he poured God's goodness into us!' Now that's an unbelievable bargain you don't want to pass up; He exchanged my sinfulness for His righteousness."

That's just one of the foundational truths that reinforce the fact that for Him, it's a "love thing." There are a whole host of foundational truths in God's word.

These foundational truths are ones we, as people of faith, should continue to remember, recall, repeat, and rehearse—the knowledge of who we are by the grace of God. These verses help us to see His perspective and the choices He made in pursuing us.

~✧~

"I am a new creation in Christ."
(2 Corinthians 5:17 NIV)

~✧~

"I am a co-heir with Christ."
(Romans 8:17 NIV)

~✧~

"I am more than a conqueror through Him who loves me."
(Romans 8:37 NIV)

~✧~

"I overcame the enemy by the blood of the lamb."
(Revelation 12:11 NIV)

~✧~

"I have everything I need to live a godly life, and I am equipped to live in His divine nature." (2 Peter 1:3-4 NIV)

~✧~

"I am the righteousness of God;
I have right standing with Him in Jesus Christ."
(2 Corinthians 5:21 NIV)

~✧~

"My body is a temple of the Holy Spirit; I belong to Him.
(1 Corinthians 6:19 NIV)

~✧~

"I am the light of the world.
(Matthew 5:14 KJV)."

~✧~

"I am chosen by God, forgiven and justified through Christ.
(Romans 8:33 NIV)

~✧~

"I am redeemed, forgiven of all my sins, and made clean through the blood of Christ. (Ephesians 1:7 NIV)

~✧~

"I am greatly loved by God.
(John 3:16 NASB)

~✧~

"He is merciful to me."
(Ephesians 2:4 NIV; Colossians 3:12 NIV)

~✧~

"I've been chosen by Him."
(1 Thessalonians 1:4 NIV)

~✧~

"I am strengthened with all power according to His glorious might".
(Colossians 1:11 NIV)

~✧~

"I am not ruled by fear because the Holy Spirit lives in me
and gives me His power, love, and self-control."
(2 Timothy 1:7 NIV)

~✧~

"The Bible teaches that His thoughts for you are more than the grains of
sand on the seashore."
(Psalm 139:17-18 NIV)

~✧~

In His Word, He calls you "a chosen child" and "the apple of His eye." Such great love and amazing grace.

What you just read is a small sample of the foundational truths found in God's word that identify who you truly are. In the act of rebuilding your life, you must start on a firm foundation. The apostle Paul refers to Christ as our "firm foundation." His truths about our identity help us recognize our true potential. It's been said, "God doesn't make junk." The very theme of this book is one of identity. You are not just a random conglomeration of active cells that evolved from apes to gain knowledge, understanding, wisdom, and purpose, only to die, adding ashes to the earth. No, you are a child of God, created with a mission, a purpose, and a reason. It's a holy identity—one that gives adventure and excitement to your very existence.

In the world of architectural design, buildings typically have three unique components: the **capstone**, the **keystone**, and the **cornerstone**. These types of stones perform different functions in the design of the building. **Capstones** are on the top of a masonry wall, where the water runs off the roof. A **keystone** is a wedge-shaped stone at the center of a masonry arch. It helps distribute the weight of both sides of the arch; typically, it's decorative, adding significance to the appearance of the building. Then there's the **cornerstone**; its purpose is unique compared to all others. It establishes the building's orientation and identifies its starting date, and with this stone, we celebrate the building's longevity and strength.

Now consider Christ. When we begin our relationship with Him, we get a fresh start, a new beginning; our new lives have a new starting date. He also reorients our reason for being. Now, with holy directives, you begin a holy conquest, able to celebrate His strength in us and a renewed vigor for life. We build on that foundation; it's solid, free of debris, able to stand the test of time, enduring forever. I've known businesses that have started on a faulty foundation, cluttered with jealousy, bitterness, envy, and anger.

Starting a plan or project with spite or covetousness is not the best way to begin anything. It's for that reason, in part, that there are non-compete laws to stop you from building on someone else's clients or the success of your last employer without their permission. I believe it is best practice to establish a business on fresh ideas, innovation, and creativity. The apostle Paul purposed to build on "no other foundation." When you steal someone else's ideas, plans, or clients, you compromise the integrity of your vision. Trust that God will bless you and your mission when you start your journey on a solid foundation.

HOW CAN EMBRACING GOD'S PERFECT
LOVE AND GUIDANCE TRANSFORM YOUR
APPROACH TO THE CHALLENGES AND
DECISIONS YOU FACE DAILY?

07

WHO AM I TRULY?

Let's now move from seeing the wide view of our spiritual landscape to zooming in on the individual heart and soul within each of us. Here, we peel back the layers of our external behaviors and deep-seated nature to uncover the essence of who we are beneath it all, guided by the transformative power of God. Through this, we aim to grasp not just how God sees us but how we can see ourselves in a new light—full of grace, purpose, and a new identity forged in divine love.

The glory of God is perfection! And no one is perfect; we all fall short. In this book, I hope that you will discover your true self, who you truly are. However, at some point, if you ever expect to experience lasting change, it's going to require the equivalent of a spiritual hard drive upgrade, with the kind of software that allows you the freedom to make wise choices, unencumbered by the dominance of your natural sinful nature. Let's call it a "Holy Upgrade."

In practical terms, before the upgrade, you might feel lost, empty, broken, lustful, greedy, deceitful, unfaithful, a natural liar, and a cheat. Should I go on? You get the picture. After the upgrade, you're spiritually found, full, blessed, compassionate, other-centered, honest, reliable, and trusted—you are someone people enjoy being around! You're sought out and valued.

Jesus had a term for it; He called it "born again." It is a brand-new perspective, a new identity, and a new internal power that comes from an Almighty source. There will be more on this at the end of the book, but it is imperative that we touch on it now. I want you to become more self-aware and include the basic knowledge of why we humans behave the way we do.

God shows us in His word, using the children of Israel as an example to us, that we must navigate through the "wilderness to get to the promised land." In their attempt to get out of Egypt and into the Holy Land, they faced trials, cultural conflict, enemy attacks, and the natural failings that come from fatigue on such a long, arduous journey.

Israel becomes a valuable illustration for us. The moment we invite God to have authority over our lives, our salvation is secure. It's at that same time that the sanctification process begins; that's the course of action the Holy Spirit integrates into our daily lives as we are conformed into a better version of ourselves. Walking with God is a daily adventure as we adjust to a new way of living. Trust me; there will be some stumbling, some falling, some running ahead, even some lagging behind, yet all along the journey, He won't let go, continuing with you, hand in grace-filled hand.

Now, let's combine God's truths about who we are with our burning desire to learn as a child. We mentioned earlier how important change is. If there is something we learned quite quickly as children, it's that seasons change. And although there are four seasons—winter, spring, summer, and fall—each one begins and ends in God's direction. You cannot predict the weather or when summer really starts in the state of Indiana. I don't think it ever started on the first day of summer, according to the calendar date, and I remember it snowing in October when the calendar said it was still fall.

The Bible puts it this way:

"There is a time for everything and a season for every activity under the heavens." (Ecclesiastes 3:1 NIV)

I'm convinced that you are in a season of life right now, and as you've made more aware of how your past has molded and shaped you, you're also more aware of how you can actively be involved in molding and shaping a better plan for tomorrow. You will agree that the positive end effect of our time together with this book could impact your marriage, your family, your business, your health, and every other part of your existence.

Seasons are not truly scheduled by the calendar date; they are scheduled according to God's direction and timing. It's often said that His timing is perfect.

Just think,
you're here not by chance,
but by God's choosing.
His hand formed you
and made you the person you are.
He compares you to no one else.
You are one of a kind.
You lack nothing
that His grace can't give you.
He has allowed you to be here
at this time in history
to fulfill His special purpose
for this generation.
—Roy Lessin

REFLECTING ON YOUR CURRENT SEASON
OF LIFE, HOW CAN UNDERSTANDING
YOUR PAST AND EMBRACING GOD'S
TRANSFORMATIVE POWER SHAPE A
BETTER PLAN FOR YOUR FUTURE?

08

DO YOU VALUE TIME?

As we transition from understanding our spiritual journey and identity in God, let's pause and reflect on how we use our precious gift called time. This chapter challenges us to think about how we can make the most of our days, live with limited regrets, and truly value the gift of every moment. Let's explore the importance of cherishing time, learning from our experiences, and using our days wisely to fulfill our God-given purpose.

Time is one of the most valuable things we have in this life. It is limited; none of us knows how much time we have. Therefore, it should be cherished and treated as a daily gift from God—a valued commodity! When we were young, we seemed to believe that we had all the time in the world, and then suddenly, we realized we had fewer days ahead than we did behind us.

When we ask a child how old they are, they often add a 1/2-year mark. They're not just three years old; they're 3 and 1/2. After our 40s, we would rather say we're "40-something." When we get to our 50s, we discover it's not even polite to ask a woman how old she is.

In a recent survey, people in their 80s were asked, if given the opportunity to live life again, what they would do differently. To summarize their answers: "Stop worrying, start living." There are no quick fixes. But instead, start planning today, start doing today—today! I know we all don't want to hear that, but just like planting seeds for a harvest and having to wait for them to grow, it takes time. Everything worthwhile has a timeline and a process.

You may be wondering if there is anything or anyone that could help you save some time that you may have lost. What if you could connect with someone or, even better, a group of people who have gained wisdom through the challenges and difficulties of life? And what if you could invite them into your space to encourage, exhort, and even coach you? Their guidance and willingness to share years of trial and error could shorten your learning curve. If you are willing to be teachable, there would certainly be a big advantage.

Before you go any further in the book, I want you to Google something: "life's greatest regrets." You will find list after list. They will include being more loving to people who matter most, being a better parent or spouse, spending too much time working, and taking better care of their bodies. And it's sad to see that when it's too late to make meaningful changes, it's too late to make meaningful changes. Let's live your life with fewer or no regrets.

I've seen the pendulum swing to both sides; some people have no problem wasting time, while others seize every minute like it is their last one to live. Ecclesiastes 7 records for us insights from Solomon's mind as he reflects on life's meaning and purpose. Verse one reads: "A good reputation is more valuable than the most expensive perfume, the day one dies is better than the day he's born, it's better to spend your time at funerals than at festivals, for you're going to die and it's good to think about it while there's still time, sorrow is better than laughter for sadness has a refining influence on us. Yes, a wise man thinks much of death while the fool thinks only of having a good time now." In verse 10, he states: "Don't long for the good old days, for you don't know whether they were any better than these."

Too much of life is spent bewailing how good it used to be, how bad it is now, how we wish it were different, and then doing nothing about it. If you're going to move forward, you must let go of the past. Your past will always follow you; it will even do its best to catch up to you and force you to stay there in the past. You will have to be the one who lets it go.

Ephesians 5:15-17 says:

"Be very careful, then, how you live—not as unwise but as wise, making the most of every opportunity because the days are evil. Therefore, do not be foolish, but understand what the Lord's will is."

Have you ever noticed that you really do nothing to keep your heart beating; it just beats? No conscious thought or effort on your part—your ticker ticks. In most cases, the day it stops ticking is not up to you; the switch is flipped. You're done.

I've always wished there was an expiration date on my body, a place with the day, month, and year. I have to wonder—if I actually knew the day and the hour, how differently I would live. I also wonder if I did know if I would procrastinate and hesitate to do the things that matter more, believing I still had time. This I do know—that I don't know the day or the hour. It's for this reason we have the apostle Paul's admonition to make the most of every opportunity, every minute, every moment, and use them wisely.

DO I REALLY NEED A COACH?

Just as we understand the value of each tick of the clock, recognizing the potential in ourselves calls for a helping hand. This next chapter transitions us from solo reflection to considering the power of partnership in our personal, professional, and spiritual development.

It's about acknowledging that sometimes; to unlock our full potential and navigate the blind spots of our journey, we might need a coach—someone who can guide, inspire, and push us beyond what we thought was possible into the realms of our true calling and deeper fulfillment. A coach's role is not just to correct or instruct but to illuminate paths we might not see, to challenge us to strive higher, and to provide the accountability we often lack when setting out alone. Through their expertise and experience, a coach can be the catalyst for change, transformation, and, ultimately, a more purposeful and impactful life.

The need for a coach is undeniable. Many of the highest-paid C-suite executives, professional athletes, singers, and actors have coaches. They all invited someone into their lives who helped them reach a goal greater than what would have been achieved alone by their own ability; so much more was accomplished with their assistance. All of us have blind spots; a coach is someone in your life who sees what you can't see because it's in your blind spot. For most of us, the last time we had a coach was in high school or college.

Sadly, when we bid farewell to school, we often said goodbye to those influences as well. However, the need still exists today. It's a sure way to maximize results. One of the most valuable sayings I've ever heard is, "Don't listen to what people say; watch what they do." You will learn more about a person by watching what they do than you will ever learn by listening to what they say. Wouldn't it make more sense to learn from people experienced in their field who are willing to roll up their sleeves and get to work with you? Somebody on your side. A true coach will help you discover your identity and your ultimate purpose. An important question to ask yourself right now is: Are you living a life driven by spiritual purpose, or are you living a life driven by selfish pleasure?

When we look at our lives as adults, we realize that our gifts, talents, and abilities have all been divinely designed with our ultimate purpose in mind. Pursuing our lives with a spiritual purpose adds joy to the journey. In most cases, when we chase pleasure to fill our voids, it's because we want to feel good. But at times, we may be avoiding or even neglecting our spiritual purpose. For example, when we are looking for love, true love—the kind of love that we were designed to enjoy—lust sneaks in; we are suddenly seduced into the quick fix. A short-term need is met that, in reality, keeps the real thing at a distance. Deluded by the phony, we waste our time and energy. Trapped, surprised by the pain, the counterfeit, selfish pleasure took the place of spiritual purpose.

To understand fulfillment and true satisfaction, we need to develop specific, detailed plans that will help us follow through with action, serve the people around us, and build a personal relationship with our Creator. Once that comes into focus with the blueprint provided in this book, we believe you will be better equipped to create and determine a more effective plan that prioritizes your own action steps and helps you get results—the kind of results that make for a more meaningful and fruitful journey.

HOW CAN A COACH HELP YOU OVERCOME YOUR JOURNEY'S BLIND SPOTS AND GUIDE YOU TOWARDS FULFILLING YOUR TRUE POTENTIAL AND SPIRITUAL PURPOSE?

10

WHY CAN'T I WING IT?

After considering the benefits of having a coach—someone to guide us and highlight what we might not see—I'm now preparing you with a clear warning and caution against the negative delusion of saying, "Why can't I wing it?" It's like moving from having someone show you the ropes to questioning why you can't just improvise your way through life.

Here, we are tackling the very temptation to take life as it comes without a plan or purpose and seeing where we might end up if we resist the structured guidance a coach offers. It's a look into the risks of the laid-back approach versus the rewards of being purposeful and planned.

No winging it! We cannot live our lives like a leaf on a tree blowing in the breeze, waiting to see where the wind takes us—no. Success happens by choice, not chance. This will require faith! You will sense a clarion call deep within your being. You will know that now is the time for courage, boldness, effort, and a desire to no longer live in the mediocrity of the status quo.

You could close this book right now, think you're not qualified, and live another empty, unfulfilling year on the planet—unchanged, unchallenged, unfulfilled, and wasting more time! Just hoping you hit the lottery. Maybe you've done that in the past—started a book, knowing it was time for a change, but like so many of your New Year's resolutions, golf lessons, gym memberships, or dance classes, you started with hope and ended in defeat.

Really, again? Seriously, you can't do that! It's time to adjust your thinking. Thomas Edison was known for saying:

"I have not failed. I've just found 10,000 ways that won't work."

Failure is not truly a failure. It is what you learn that becomes your roadmap to success. Failure only happens when you give fear greater power over choosing to try again. It's best if you make a mistake and make the necessary adjustments for another attempt.

Stop for a minute and look at your index finger. Do you see that print on the tip? That's yours, no one else's. You are the only person in the world with that print. Consider your eye—your retina has a pattern that is exclusive to you. No one else in the world has ever had the same pattern as you. The same is true with your vein pattern; again, it's exclusively yours. An X-ray of your body would reveal that the way your veins are aligned, outside of your skeleton inside your flesh, is unique to you.

I'm convinced that your fingers were designed to touch the world as only you could, your eyes to see the things that God wants you to see, and your veins to course through your body and move you into a groove—a path that God foreordained before the creation of the world, one that you would walk in His will and discover a life with a true ultimate purpose. We all have different gifts, talents, and abilities to fulfill our ultimate purpose. Your DNA, I believe, is God's Divine Nonnegotiable Agenda. The uniqueness of you is true in everyone's life. One person may write the movie, but it takes hundreds to get the movie made. Yes, there's a writer, but there's also a producer, a director, stagehands, lighting crews—the list goes on. And when the movie comes to an end, you see hundreds of names—every gifted person in their line of work who helped make that movie a blockbuster.

The same is true with music; there's a writer, a producer, musicians, a promoter, a salesman—the list goes on. Michael Jackson would not have been such a success had it not been for Quincy Jones. There were four Beatles, not one. The combination of Tom Brady and Bill Belichick made for an undeniable force, leading the New England Patriots to championship after championship. Had it not been for the Wright brothers, the plane would never have gotten off the ground. The size of the average football team is much larger than the group that is ready on the field. You have heard it said, "There is no *I* in team."

When God created Adam and Eve, one of His main directives was that they "go forth, be fruitful, and multiply." Basically, he commanded that they "go make some people"—populate the planet. When you attempt to do life as a solo act, you limit the resources of a great supporting cast that God has created to assist you and help motivate you—those providential people who will be used to take you to higher heights and greater goals.

WHAT STEPS COULD YOU TAKE TODAY
TO MOVE AWAY FROM "WINGING IT" AND
TOWARDS A MORE PURPOSEFUL AND
PLANNED APPROACH TO ACHIEVING
YOUR GOALS?

11

WHO IS CALLED TO LEAD?

Continuing forward from the clear realization that we can't just "wing it" through life, we step into a new realm of questioning: Who is called to lead? It's a thought that can catch us off guard. Leadership isn't about having all the answers or being perfect. It's about stepping up, even when you feel least qualified.

Ask yourself, "Could I be called to lead?" Have you ever wondered if you could be the one called to make a difference? Let's see how we might be called to light the way for others.

For years, a friend of mine had a plaque on the wall in his office that said, "God does not call the qualified; He qualifies the called." This divine guidance is a comforting truth. We've all known someone who's in a leadership role, and it doesn't seem to fit—maybe nepotism or they just couldn't find the right person for the job, so they filled the spot. So, what about you? Could you be called? You might be asking yourself, what do you mean? I mean, what if God calls you? Yes, you! You could ignore it—go ahead, try to neglect His leading. I guess you could try to run away from the opportunity, but you can't run from Him. Do you really think you can outrun God? I'm thinking He's faster! You could fight it, but ultimately, He wins, so why would you? Consider this: according to God's word, His will for your life is "good, pleasing, and perfect" (Romans 12:2 NIV).

It's highly unlikely you're going to enjoy your path more than His. You're a light to the world, and you have been divinely designed to shine. Every person who accepts Christ is called to influence others. God knows what He's doing; He knows who He is calling. Everything in life is connected to your calling. Until you uncover the fullness of what you were created for, you will find yourself frustrated.

Why frustrated? Let me explain with a simple golf club example. Those who design golf clubs do so with a very specific spot on the face of the club called a "sweet spot." When you line up the ball just as the designers intended and hit it right on that "sweet spot," the ball will fly effortlessly into the sky, going further and faster, exactly as the creators of the club intended. You will feel like a pro! You will have a renewed passion for the game and excitement to play again.

In the same way, God designed you with a "sweet spot"—a place etched on your being, where your natural God-given talents and skills can make the biggest impact and grant you the most meaning and reason for your existence. Wouldn't you want to answer the call of God in your life rather than pursue a mundane, less satisfying career? This journey of self-discovery and growth is what makes leadership so inspiring and motivating.

Leadership is a character quality; your life is exemplary, and naturally, others follow. Influence is different; everyone influences. It doesn't require character; media platforms are filled with influencers. For a variety of reasons, both good and bad, today's influencers are popular people with a large following. Often, their character is questionable; they are not followed for their morality or their lack of compromise in life. Some of the most famous influencers are rude, mean, antagonistic, and self-absorbed. Do you remember your mother telling you to stay away from the kid down the block because he was a bad influence on you? A good leader should have integrity, self-awareness, courage, respect, empathy, and gratitude.

These qualities can be learned and improved upon; with a willing heart and some holy guidance, you can become the person that others will choose to follow—that's leadership.

Be mindful that a LEADER LEADS. They have COURAGE. They make a CHOICE to be DISCIPLINED and FOCUSED. They also create a PLAN to accomplish the GOALS of their desired OUT-COMES. This emphasis on discipline and focus is what sets leaders apart and should inspire a sense of determination and commitment in their audience.

Again, remember that with God's help, we can gain control over what we think and how we act. So, let's examine our lives through a unique blueprint designed for Healthy Living—The 4D Method.

IF LEADERSHIP IS ABOUT INFLUENCING OTHERS, IN WHAT WAYS DO YOU SEE YOURSELF ALREADY IMPACTING THOSE AROUND YOU? HOW CAN YOU EXPAND ON THESE INFLUENCES?

Two

DEFINE & DESIGN

Design must reflect the practical and the aesthetic in business but above all... good design must primarily SERVE PEOPLE.
Thomas J. Watson

12

HOW HEALTHY AM I?

Discovering The 4D Method

"Do you not know that in a race, all the runners run, but only one gets the prize? Run in such a way as to get the prize."
1 Corinthians 9:24 (NIV)

Let's now delve into a more personal inquiry: How fit are we for the journey of life ahead of us? This next chapter, "How Healthy Am I," prompts us to examine our health and well-being. It's a reminder that whether we're steering a business or team, managing a family, or simply trying to lead a fulfilling life, our physical, mental, financial, and relational development plays a critical role in our overall success. Like the finely tuned athletes in Formula One racing, our success and ability to reach our goals are closely tied to how well we take care of ourselves. Let's take a moment to check in with ourselves, understanding that to lead effectively, we need to be in our best shape, ready for the race of life.

Each year, only 20 men are hand-picked to represent Formula One racing, the most prestigious racing circuit in the world. The cars they drive are worth between 12 to 15 million dollars each. With ten teams and two drivers on each team, the competition is high-adrenaline, extremely tense, and physically grueling. These drivers must be incredibly fit, on their game, and laser focused. It's a 90-minute, once-a-week job. Their income for this work ranges from 5 million to 60 million per year before endorsements and royalties. But did you know they all have trainers for their bodies, counselors, and therapists for their minds and emotions, as well as agents to help them with their income and investments? They also have families with strong bonds to walk with and talk with as they travel through the ups and downs of this constant competition. If you plan to win, it will never be a solo sport.

The rigorous discipline and effort invested in this sport is for a prize that will not last forever. On the other hand, a Christian pursues a lasting reward. Just as racers undergo strict training for a perishable prize, Christians aim for an imperishable crown promised by God. This commitment to faith and the teachings of the Bible guides us toward a prize that endures forever, urging us to align our lives with the eternal objectives set by Christ.

There are four basic dimensions, areas, or quadrants of development in which we move, work, live, learn, and play every day. Several factors impact and influence each dimension, and each area needs to be paid attention to and maintained for maximum performance.

The 4D Method: Four Dimensions of Development for Healthy Living

1. M.E.C. Health (Mental. Emotional. Cognitive)

2. Physical Health

3. Financial Health

4. Relational Health

You can use this information just like you use the information that you get from a doctor when you go for your annual physical. Most of us resist going to the doctor unless we're in pain. Pain is an amazing motivator. We may neglect or ignore this regular physical checkup because we feel fine, but the medical world will tell you time and time again that with the early diagnosis of any disease, the hope of arresting the disease or eradicating the disease increases exponentially when detected early. In much the same way, if we're honest with ourselves and we have anger issues, it would be best to harness them now before they grow into an act of rage where the consequences are far greater.

CONSIDERING THE 4D METHOD, WHICH AREA OF YOUR HEALTH DO YOU THINK NEEDS THE MOST ATTENTION RIGHT NOW AND WHY?

THE FOUR DIMENSIONS OF DEVELOPMENT FOR HEALTHY LIVING

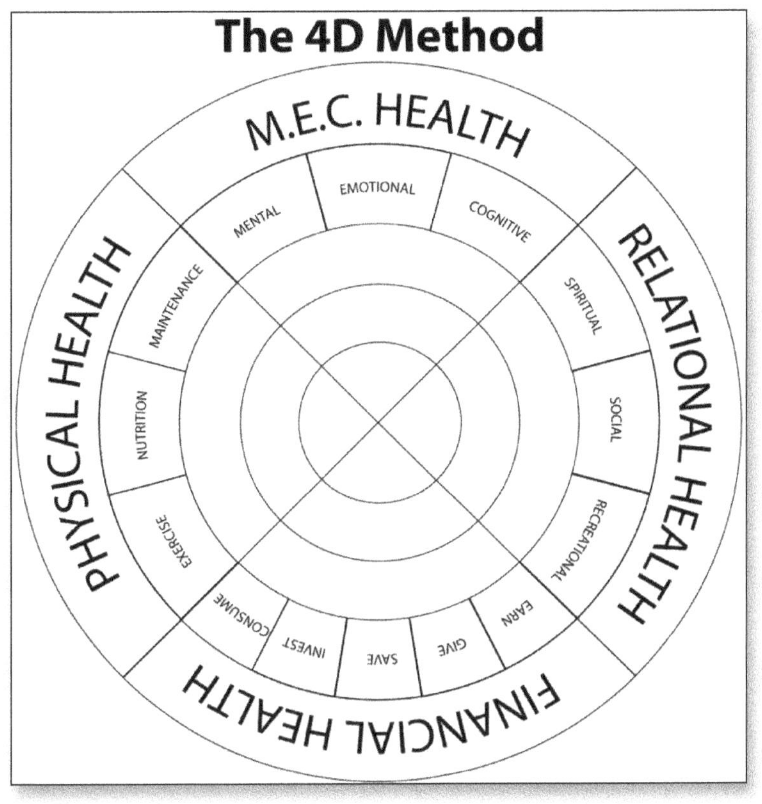

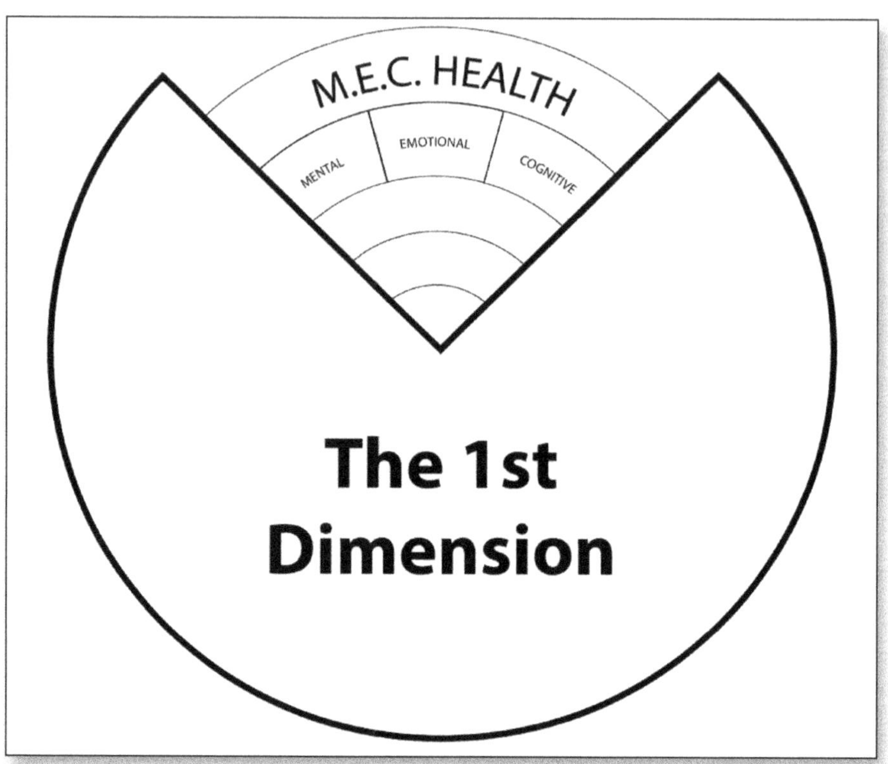

M.E.C. Health- Mental, Emotional, and Cognitive Health.

The word "head" is commonly used to describe the place of greatest influence: the head of a corporation, the head of the house, the head of a hammer. When you "hit it on the head," you find the ultimate target. The mind is where we must begin—the place where your thoughts are incubated, considered, debated, and chewed. Anything that happens in your life starts with a choice, a decision, and that is ignited in your head. It serves the body as an information processing center. All the rest of your body's sensors check with your brain first to decide what's next. The importance of a healthy mind cannot be understated. Your brain is not a muscle; it's an organ—one that actually plays a huge role in controlling muscles throughout your body.

The apostle Paul in 1 Timothy 4:7-8 (N.I.V.) urged us "to exercise ourselves toward godliness." Just as the muscles in your body naturally atrophy—losing their elasticity and strength when you choose not to move—so too can your spiritual and mental faculties weaken without proper exercise. Your mind has control over your muscles; it all starts with the decision to get up, to get moving, and to take control.

We often fall into what I call the "analysis that leads to paralysis." We sit around thinking about what we should do and could do, yet we don't take action. Our minds can be filled with visions, thoughts, plans, hopes, and dreams, but it's not until we begin to actively pursue them, with plans in hand, that we will see a difference. While I am not a doctor and make no medical claims, I can speak from personal experience: by adopting certain principles and practices, I have seen dramatic, lifelong changes that sharpen our skills, talents, and abilities.

Here are the definitions of M.E.C.

a) **Mental health** is the ability to think clearly and make good decisions. It's often associated with a person's overall mental well-being. It affects how we think, feel, and act. It also helps determine how we handle stress, relate to others, and make healthy choices.

b) **Emotional health** is the ability to cope with and manage emotions; it's also the ability to have positive relationships. It involves maintaining a balanced outlook on how we think and feel. It's about our sense of well-being, our mood and feelings, our ability to cope with life events, and how we acknowledge our own emotions without self-serving drama or awkward outbursts. Even assisting others with a compassionate and helpful disposition is part of emotional stability, which is an asset.

c) **Cognitive health** is an active brain that can perform all the mental processes collectively known as cognition, including the ability to learn new things, intuition, judgment, language, and memory. Cognitive health is just one aspect of overall brain health.

Since thoughts are ingredients and we should be able to control our thinking, how do we consistently influence and even enhance M.E.C. health to make something better in our lives? In other words, how do we prioritize the information we consume?

I have done a lot of hiring, and some of the questions I love to ask reveal and expose character conditions that help me assess the candidate. One question is: What's on your nightstand? Is there anything you're reading right now or a podcast you're listening to? I want to discover if there's anything they're doing to increase their productivity, make changes in their lives, and influence their well-being. How about you?

Consider the following when prioritizing what you allow yourself to consume:

Books and literature: What are you reading? A novel or fiction? Do you like history? The gateway to your mind can be a very adventurous place; you can travel, kick a habit, prepare for future opportunities, or even learn a second language. You should treat it as a high-value space—don't let just anything live there. It has such important value.

Videos: Have you ever binge-watched a dramatic series that has so captured your attention that you can't stop? Your eye gate is digesting images; some you'll forget, and some will stay. I like to think of my video viewing as like a menu at a restaurant: I need something of substance, call it my meat and potatoes, but I look forward to dessert. However, if all I digest is the sweet stuff, the ill effects of my choices may hinder some exciting growth in my life.

Audio: The ear gate provides access to all the frequencies and sounds of life—from whispered voices, waves crashing, birds singing, babies crying, police sirens, and radio waves. It's also another place of revelation like your other senses. You can learn a lot about yourself by your general awareness of what you like to hear; your preferences become indicators of what you enjoy and what you dislike. Certain sounds can fill your mind with memories and can create or recreate events; a song from your past can bring you right back to the high school prom or a marching band, and you're back at the game. The list for listening is endless, but with the advent of podcasts, I don't know how many of us truly recognize what a tool the ear is to educate and inform. Listening is learning.

Environments: This is your place and your space—your condo, house, apartment, your crib. Your surroundings educate and affect a large part of who you are. It's why we take vacations, road trips, and even a Saturday walk on the beach. We've all heard somebody say, "I just want to get away from it all." It's a cry for a different scene, a different location, believing that the change of physical proximity will affect their mood and disposition. Location, location, location—I'm sure you've heard it's everything!

Prayer and Meditation: I've found that the most balanced, organized, and peaceful people are those who make it a habit to pause and reflect regularly. They create intentional moments to interrupt the often hectic and chaotic flow of life, giving themselves space to consider what truly matters. This pause allows them to contemplate what is necessary, what is non-negotiable, what holds the most value, and what can be discarded. My father used to say, "Son, common sense is not so common." Common sense, by definition, is the ability to perceive and respond to external stimuli with sound judgment. What we take in through our senses—what we see, hear, feel, taste, and smell—becomes part of us, influencing our thoughts and actions. It's vital to use our senses deliberately, discerning what we truly value because what we absorb shapes our current state and can be used to create a more favorable future. Ask yourself: Are you growing in understanding your life, your purpose, and your reason for being? Remember, we are lifelong learners.

Fellowship: In the Bible, fellowship refers to a kind of camaraderie that is much more than a backyard B.B.Q., catching up on someone else's kids and talking ball scores. The word in Greek is Koinonia; it describes a connection that is encouraging, stimulating, and spiritual as the common values of the Christian faith are discussed and enjoyed. I relish connecting with people of faith and having the kind of conversations that leave me better off than before they began. Proverbs 27:17 (N.L.T.) says, "As iron sharpens iron, so a friend sharpens a friend." Use a pencil too long, and it gets dull. The lead soon disappears, and some of us attempt to write with a wooden nub—ineffective and unintelligible.

The same can be said about our life. We need a sharpener—a friend, a companion, someone who's willing to come alongside and champion our cause. I meet regularly with a group of guys; we meet to encourage, stimulate, and exhort one another in the most positive ways. I'm always disappointed when it ends. The Bible teaches there is safety in a multitude of counselors. It doesn't say there is direction in a multitude of counselors—God alone should be directing your life. However, it is safe and smart to balance and bounce your bigger decisions off those who know you and care about the general direction of your life. The word "sharpen" in the above text literally means that sparks will fly during the sharpening process. I will pray that while you read this, you'll wisely select a few folks in your life who will help you stay sharp and focused on the goals you set forth.

It may be a rather dramatic illustration to make a point, but I can still recall the cause of the horrific catastrophe of Korean Air Lines Flight 007 on September 1, 1983. The Boeing 747 was routed from Anchorage to Seoul, but the crew made a navigational mistake. The airliner drifted off course and flew through Soviet-prohibited airspace. A total of 269 lives were lost; the cause was that the navigation tracker was off by just 3 degrees—not much when you think of it. But just 3 degrees when taking off becomes more with every mile you travel.

The Soviet military, thinking they were spies, took it down. We must get this truth deep into our souls: Being off just a little, if not checked, can be more dangerous than you think. Jesus asked, "What does it profit a man if he gains the whole world but forfeits his soul?" Notice He didn't say body or even spirit, but He used the word "soul." That's the place of your God-given identity, your meaning, your definition, your reason for being.

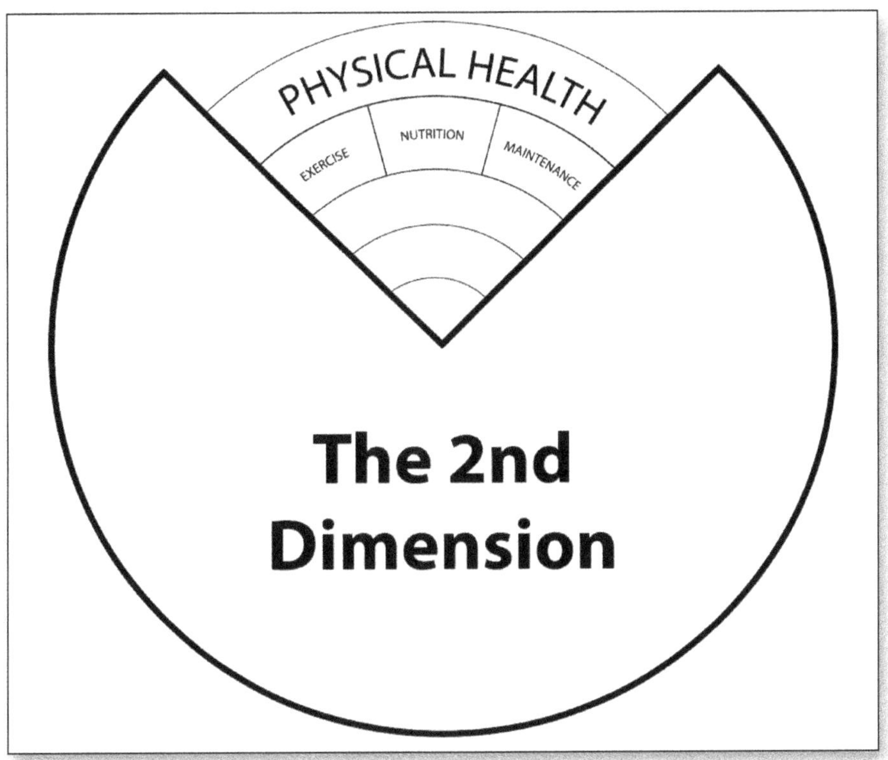

PHYSICAL HEALTH

Temple care is the attention given to the vehicle in which your soul and Spirit reside.

> *"Don't you realize that your body is the temple of the Holy Spirit, who lives in you and was given to you by God? You do not belong to yourself, for God bought you with a high price. So, you must honor God with your body."*
> *1 Corinthians 6:19–20 (NLT)*

Below are three areas (Exercise, Nutrition, Maintenance) that are broken down for simple understanding which are vital to your overall well-being:

EXERCISE | Sculpting and Energy

I don't expect that you'll become a gym rat living in your local fitness center. But I do believe that to get the most out of your life, there will have to be some investment in your body. If you don't change the oil in your car, brush your teeth, or take out the trash, there will be consequences. You know the old adage: "If you don't use it, you'll lose it."

Regular physical activity is one of the most important things you can do for your health. It can improve brain health, help manage weight, reduce the risk of disease, strengthen bones and muscles, and improve your ability to do everyday activities. Not getting enough physical activity can lead to heart disease, even for people who have no other risk factors.

This is the part of the book that will be the most challenging for some people. Because you've lived with yourself for so long, you've grown accustomed to the way you look and carrying the weight you have, and every time you make an effort, you don't see an immediate change. Sadly, that's what most fitness centers count on.

In fact, up to 67% of gym memberships go completely unused. Only about 18% of members actually go to the gym consistently, and of those who actively use their gym membership, 49% go at least twice a week. It may have more to do with getting set in your ways; if your routine doesn't include any exercise, the thought of adjusting your life for the loss of a few pounds and for the lack of a few sweets doesn't do anything for you.

It's also noteworthy that the average age of gym fitness center attendees is 18 to 34. So, if you're past the age of 40, and you look in the mirror and don't see what you used to see—or maybe you've never seen it—it's more difficult to start. Maybe my encouragement needs to be along the lines of not pulling a muscle or throwing out a joint. There's nothing worse than injuring your shoulder by simply taking your briefcase or backpack out of the back seat of your car.

I believe what really needs to happen is that you take some small steps, literally small steps. It's not the five-mile run that you should start with; it's the walk around the block after dinner. Personally, I've chosen only to take stairs when practically able; you can also purchase an inexpensive fitness watch and start keeping track of how many steps you take during the day. I think you'll be surprised and encouraged, along with the added exhortation from the watch itself; you know that it's time to stand when you've been sitting too long because it's going to tell you.

Here are two straightforward areas for exercise

1. **Resistance**: As the name suggests, resistance involves opposing or fighting against something, whether through action or argument. When muscles work against a force, the effort builds beneficial tension, strengthening and elongating them. Examples include weight training with free weights or machines, utilizing resistance bands, practicing isometrics, and even humorous scenarios like changing a tire—though that's more for a chuckle unless you're actually up for it.

2. **Moving**: This involves any activity that propels your body through space. Walking, running, swimming, and stretching are key examples. Participating in sports like tennis, baseball, football, soccer, volleyball, and pickleball also counts. Essentially, if it gets you moving, it's beneficial for your body—did I really need to spell that out?

NUTRITION | Fuel & Energy

Before I list the four basic areas of nutrition, I want to share with you a two-word phrase that changed my eating habits: "acquired taste." It simply means that what you may find unfamiliar or even objectionable to eat and digest can gradually become more liked or even enjoyed.

Example: As a teenager, the thought of eating spinach would produce a gag reflex, but the more I understood its value and importance to my well-being, the more I grew to like it. Today, I enjoy spinach! Trust me when I say that if you stick to it and recognize its value and benefits, you can change the way you eat based on what you eat.

Think about the snacks you eat and choose to replace what is less healthy with something healthier. Potato chips can be replaced with more healthful choices such as dried fruit and nuts like walnuts and pistachios. And don't wait to go to the circus to get peanuts; breaking the shells can help you exercise your finger muscles. Big smile, but I'm serious.

I know it's difficult; it seems to me that the experts on nutritious foods seemingly change their opinions every year or so; it's a different opinion. A while back, they decided eggs were not that good for you; then they changed their minds, and now they're great again. It's even harder to choose a nutritional milk to drink; one month, it's soy; the next month, it's oat; another month, it's almond.

I suggest that you take the time to adjust the foods you eat so that nutrition becomes the goal. It's okay to have a cheat day. I have found personally that if I eat healthy throughout the week, when I finally get to cheat day, I'm not so much in the mood to eat something that may not settle or digest like it used to; you see, once you change those habits, the new habits take the place of the old.

Here are the four areas of nutrition for optimal health to consider:

1. **Food**: It's been said we are what we eat; too many Americans feel like junk, and it's called junk food for a reason.

2. **Water**: Lots of it; considering 70% of our body is water, we need to hydrate and replenish all the necessary fluids that are naturally depleted in the course of our day.

3. **Fasting**: Yes, it can be done. Whether it's intermittent fasting, which has become very popular in recent years, or prolonged fasting, most people are surprised at the many benefits provided to the human body simply by abstaining.

4. **Supplements**: The last time I had my blood checked, the doctor told me I was low in iron. A simple supplement changed that, and I feel better. The next time you see the physician, check for yourself; you might be missing something that you could truly benefit from.

MAINTENANCE | Repair and Nurture

Body care should be an experience that brings you peace, enjoyment, and relaxation. Meeting with experts in this field is very wise when it comes to maintaining your health, including your general self-image. These experts have spent years focused on this one particular part of your well-being. It doesn't matter what type of doctor—holistic or medical, dentist, chiropractor, personal trainer, massage therapist, or nutritionist—you consult; respect must be given to people whose sole purpose is to make you better.

Of course, we can all have opinions and favorites, and that is different for everyone because we all have a unique body with unique needs. This is a personal journey that should not be neglected. When you can turn off the world and soak for half an hour in the tub with some music playing, you'll be surprised how refreshed you will feel.

A massage will do wonders for your body and your mind. If you have access to a swimming pool, you don't have to do laps. Just float, move your arms a bit, your legs a little; trust me, you'll be glad you did this. The way you feel about yourself impacts and influences your expression.

I have a friend who had crooked teeth from childhood; in his 40s, he decided to get braces. Today, there's Invisalign. As a sales rep for a large company, it had a profound effect on the way he greeted clients with the confidence of his smile. Your clothing also affects not only the way that others see you but also the way you see yourself. An inexpensive, well-tailored suit is better than an expensive suit that doesn't fit. It's the little things that can make a difference.

A walk on the beach, a new pillow that gives you a better night's sleep, or a back massage. The new rage is a cold plunge, proven to reduce muscle soreness, improve your general mood, boost your metabolism, and strengthen your immune system. I'm convinced that after that, you would definitely be sharper and more alert; certainly, it would snap you out of your normal morning funk.

In junior high school, there was a kid in my English class who used to say to the teacher on a regular basis, in a very whiny tone, "I don't feel like it." The rest of the kids in class would snicker and giggle. Obviously, there were times when none of us felt like it, but getting a good grade wasn't about feelings; it was more about shaking off your slack attitude and doing the work.

There are things you can do to make a difference. But if you "don't feel like it," well, for the kid in class, his lack of feeling meant a failing grade. As adults, we grow out of a feeling-based disposition; there are a lot of things I don't feel like doing. I don't feel like taking out the trash or doing the laundry. I've never been excited about doing the dishes. Growing up is also growing out of that lackadaisical attitude that leaves us stalled in the same place and in the same condition year after year.

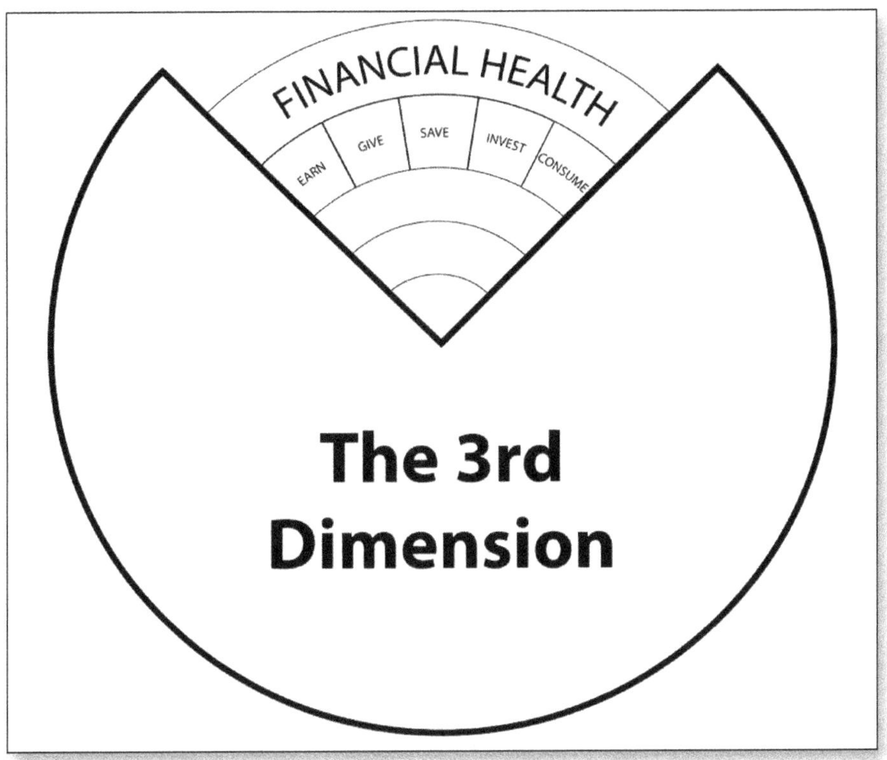

FINANCIAL HEALTH - How to Rightly View Money

Let's learn how to use money properly and make it work for us instead of chasing it. Learning to see our finances as tools is critical to a healthy life. If we become too emotionally attached to money, we are more likely to make mistakes and be led astray by never-ending money-making propositions. A proper perspective is important here, as it helps us sort out all the confusion about our finances.

Sadly, it's often believed that if we have enough money, all our worries and troubles will go away. The problem is that the most valuable things in life that money can't buy are time, fulfillment, inner peace, integrity, true love, character, manners, a cancer-free body, respect, morals, trust, patience, class, or common sense. The things in life that should matter more should never be neglected for the things that matter less. Be reminded that the Word of God tells us that the "love of money is the root of all kinds of evil."

Those who have lived long enough have seen that fact play out time and time again. Notice that it's the "love" of money that is the root of evil; that's the trap, not money itself. Money is a tool, something that should and can be used to bless others, change lives, and create a life rich in meaning and purpose—a holy heritage for future generations. Your desire for more should be linked to a desire for more substance, not just more stuff, and your motivation should be more about leveraging your skills and talents to make the most of your life rather than greedily pursuing ill-gotten gains, only to discover that such acquisitions lead to a more frustrated and shallow life.

Money is the ultimate magnifier. For people who are super kind and generous, money will make them kinder and more generous. For those who are selfish and stingy, those attributes will only increase. While money isn't the root of a happy life, it will certainly magnify the things already present in a person's life.

The following is an outline to help you define your financial health blueprint. As you read, think about what applies to you, but also consider what may apply to others that you are not aware of. This list will also provide possible areas of growth in your personal financial portfolio. For any personal questions that you are looking for answers to, you can reach out by email at:

admin@iammasterpiece.com.

We are here to inform, educate, and provide the resources necessary to succeed with The 4D Method.

There are five main ingredients in building wealth: Earning, Consuming, Saving, Investing, and Giving. Let's check them out now.

1. **Earning**

   Do you have a plan to acquire the money you make with the gifts and talents God gave you? As people, we miss all the shots we don't take. Wayne Gretzky was so right when he said this. When you look at wealthy people, there are usually only three differences between them and the average person.

The first is that they know their target and desired outcome. Most people know what they don't want and have no idea what they actually want. Remember, we attract what we are, not what we want.

The second difference is that they believe it is possible to achieve their desired outcome. Without belief, we, as people, end up settling for what other people want for our lives.

The third and final difference is that they take consistent, massive action toward achieving the goal. As Zig Ziglar famously said, "If you aim at nothing, you will hit it every time."

It doesn't matter whether you're an employee, an employer, or self-employed. Making a plan and taking daily action is free and actionable in any circumstance. When it comes to financial stability and growing wealth, it starts with what comes in.

2. Giving

Think of *giving* as the charitable side of your character, expressing itself through deeds and resources. The Word of God divides our charitable giving into two categories: alms and tithes. An *alm* is a donation typically given to the poor and needy. Giving alms is primarily about donating your time, money, services, or resources to others who are in great need.

Tithing is different. The word "tithe" comes from Hebrew and means 10%. Today, many more contemporary churches believe tithing is only an Old Testament admonition, just for Jews. I understand the argument; however, it's still a great starting point.

We say we love God, yet statistically speaking, the unbelieving world in America, on average, gives 2% of its income to charitable work; sadly, the church is only up to 3% annually, and yet we would never think of tipping 3% at the end of a meal at our local restaurant.

The waitress would look at us, thinking, "What did I do wrong?" "Why would you treat me this way?" We struggle to give God more than 3% but tip our waiters 20%, but we really love God. Certainly, something to think about: commit to that number as a starting point and see what happens to your heart.

God has many special promises for those who live generous lives. In Judaism, it was expected that, out of their blessings from God, a minimum of 10% would return to God's house in a display of gratitude. I've always believed that giving is a true test of character. It's a clear, tangible, and specific indicator of what you truly believe. It divides the generous from the greedy and the sympathetic from the selfish.

3. **Saving**

Most people think of saving as restricting yourself to putting money in the bank. They are exactly right; however, emotionally, this can be a draining way to look at it. I prefer to think of saving as a way of paying for your future self. Ten years from now, you'll be somewhere; how you prepare now will determine where.

Putting money aside for an opportunity or emergency is a wise decision; have a line item in your budget for saving. The phrase "rainy day" comes from the fact that not every day is filled with sunshine and blessings. When the dark clouds come—as they always do—whether or not you are prepared for them will determine how you can respond.

Have you ever considered what percentage of earnings we should allocate to savings? Saving suggestions may include reducing and redirecting the money you allocate to several streaming services, such as HBO, MAX, HULU, or Disney.

How about lowering some of that Amazon spending or even quitting smoking? And what about no Starbucks? Now, I've gone too far. LOL. Well, you'll think of something. The word "decision" means to cut off from, and deciding and sticking to it can make dramatic changes in your financial future.

4. **Investing**

This is the wisest, most deliberate choice to get your money working for you. In the Parable of the Talents (Matthew 25:14-30), the wise and faithful servant put his master's money to work. Notice that the money went to work. Wisely invested money can be at work while you're sleeping. This is an exciting time!

Investments can be passive or active. For example, getting an inheritance, investing in an index fund in the stock market, or buying cash-value life insurance are all ways of investing passively.

Active investments include starting a business, buying real estate, or anything that requires your effort to make it produce money. Education and mentorship are also examples of active investments. Even getting better at your job will help you earn more money.

Simply put, investing doesn't need to be complicated. It is more about a process than a product.

5. **Consuming**

We are consumers by nature. The air we breathe and the energy we use to live all come from consumption. We need food and liquids to live. The average American digests a literal ton of food each year. Without consumption, we would cease to exist. A "carbon footprint " is the total amount of greenhouse gases that our actions generate. Simply existing on earth costs something.

What do you utilize, and what are your expenditures? Do you have a budget? What percentage of revenue should be put aside from what we earn for what we consume? These are the core questions to ask when thinking about the second step in the process of building wealth: what goes out.

When it comes to our money, we are constantly giving it away to other people. The key is understanding and controlling who we give our money to. I encourage everyone reading this to write down the ten people or businesses to whom you give the most money.

Some of the most common examples are the government, Amazon, the bank (mortgage), landlords, car companies, Verizon, Walmart, grocery stores, malls, Target, clothing companies, and airlines.

When you make the list, understand that none of these are necessarily bad. This is just something you need to be aware of. Once you know who is getting your money, you can then make a plan to redirect that money and give it to people who will help you live a better life in the future.

Lastly, increasing your income, being mindful of reducing your consumption, and being a consistent saver, investor, and giver is going to be your recipe for wealth. A friendly reminder of who you work with can make a huge difference in your opportunities for growth in all these areas.

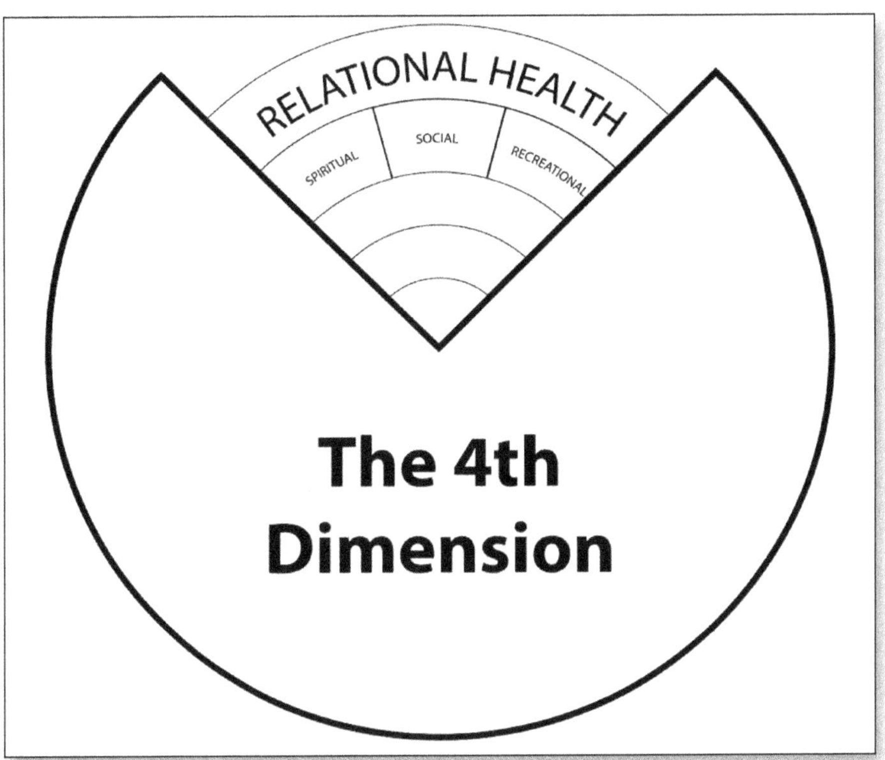

RELATIONAL HEALTH

This dimension is divided into three separate subsections. It deals with what I believe to be a hidden power that, if unpacked properly, defines our relationship with God and the rest of humanity. These next two statements are so powerful that they can affect everything in life.

Matthew 22:37-39 says, "You must love the Lord your God with all your heart, all your soul, and all your mind. This is the first and greatest commandment" (and I would add relationship). The second important thing is to "love your neighbor as yourself" (and I would echo the second important relationship). These two commandments form the basis of the entire law and all of the prophets' demands.

These simple, clear commands are the cornerstone of the health of every aspect of our lives. They clearly state how we should approach, treat, honor, cherish, defend, and pursue our relationships with everything.

Recorded in the Old Testament or the Torah, faithful Judaism required the keeping of 613 specific commands. For every Jewish person, this was a painstaking and worrisome effort to keep them righteous in God's sight. Failure to keep the law was only remedied through an animal sacrifice; with the death of your livestock came the cleansing of sin.

It, therefore, stands to reason that when Christ showed up on the scene, one of the first questions was, "Lord, what commands are we to keep?" to which Jesus responded, "You're to love the Lord your God with your heart, mind, soul, and strength, and you're to love your neighbor as yourself." He continued, "On these two commands hang all of the law and the prophets." Notice that loving God requires a strong vertical connection with your heart, which is linked to heaven in a relationship with Jesus Christ.

In the second part of that commandment, you will see a horizontal link to your fellow man. There is a direct and obvious connection between anyone who claims to follow Christ and the way they treat others in the three spheres of relational contact.

"Whoever claims to love God yet hates a brother or sister is a liar. For whoever does not love their brother and sister, whom they have seen, cannot love God, whom they have not seen." (1 John 4:20)

In light of the above text, it's clear that truly loving God will be reflected and expressed in the way that we love others.

Next, we invite you into the three parts—spiritual, social, and recreational—that make up areas of relational health:

Spiritual Health

This is your connection to God. Although there are many flavors of faith and many different denominations, the common glue that holds all of them together is our collective agreement on who Jesus is and

His access and authority in and over our lives. Traditionally, this relationship with God is experienced and expressed in four basic ways.

1. You study and read His Word. Getting to know Him is a fundamental and reasonable act of worship. God has a book out; it's been a consistent #1 seller since its inception. The Bible describes itself in many ways: bread, milk, meat, and honey, just to name a few. In the same way, we need physical food for our physical bodies; we need spiritual food to feed our spirit. Naturally, you spend time learning about and discovering the people you love; the same is true in our relationship with God.

2. Prayer is talking to God and listening to Him as the Holy Spirit guides you. You probably won't hear His voice audibly, yet you will sense when He is leading, guiding, and, yes, speaking. There is something about prayer that makes it an intimate contact with God. As people of faith, we refer to it as being in His presence; it's difficult to describe when the experience is so spiritual. But because God is supernatural, it becomes an act of fellowship with Him.

3. Fellowship is a partnership with those who also follow God; it's a blessed and encouraging aspect of your common faith when we share our experiences with like-minded people.

4. Evangelizing is the automatic conversation you have with anyone and everyone about your friendship with God. I'm really in love with my wife. It's very commonplace in everyday conversations to talk about the joy and satisfaction in my marriage. The same should be true of your relationship with God.

Social Health

One of the best indicators of your general well-being is your behavior and acceptance when you interact with other people. Your work relationships, family, friends, community, and even random providential people all contribute to your social health. Family relationships can be some of the most challenging because you're not free to choose them. If you have an argumentative sibling, they are still family, and the way you navigate the ups and downs of life is felt more dramatically in the family unit. The way you manage your workplace relationships impacts your success or failure at work.

A promotion can hinge on the way you interact with your peers. What are your social interactions like? Do you have true friends with whom you enjoy the freedom to disagree while remaining close? Proverbs 27:9 (NIV) reminds us: "Perfume and incense bring joy to the heart, and the pleasantness of a friend springs from their heartfelt advice."

Understand that the closest of friends are used to speaking into your life; they may see a blind spot, an area for improvement. Proverbs 19:20 (NIV) recommends that we "listen to advice and accept discipline, and in the end, you will be counted among the wise." Friends are often a reflection of us; the old saying "We become who we hang out with" is true; bikers hang with bikers, golfers hang with golfers, and fishermen can talk for hours with those who love to fish.

However, if you're in a season of your life where you have become isolated and somewhat disconnected from the outside world, remember that God did say, "It's not good for man to be alone." That applies not just to having a wife; it's also true about having healthy, helpful influences in our lives.

Family should be important—a true gift from God, one you should care for, be intentional with, play with, relax with, guide through life with, make time for, and listen to. If you were not raised in what we commonly call the nuclear family, our hope is that you were able to apply the basic elements of trust, loyalty, and partner relationships that, if done in the way it's intended, you also enjoyed the fruit of a family-type relationship.

Husband and wife, parents and children, siblings, extended family, stepfamily, and even family pets—you can learn a lot about people by how they care for their family animals.

Friends are those whom we trust and with whom we build relationships. They consist of single, married, widowed, and divorced people. They are outside of the family, the ones who get our time, service, and viewpoint; they impact our lives in various ways and have the power to influence our decisions more than others.

Community peers and strangers have considerable influence in our lives, sometimes even more than family and friends. A coach or teacher can affect or change the trajectory of our lives by seeing a special talent or skill. Their advice often lasts years after our initial contact. The way we interact with local law enforcement or the town council will sometimes reveal how we feel about authority figures in our lives.

Random chance providential people are those whom you don't know today, but tomorrow, they may play a very integral part in your life. God will providentially put people in your path; as the old saying goes: "When the student is ready, the teacher will appear." I have close friends today that I didn't have five years ago, and some of my closest friends, for a variety of reasons, are not as prominent in my life today. I encourage people all the time to keep their "antenna" up—you never know if the acquaintance you make today will play a much more important role in your life tomorrow. Everyday living may stir up a chance meeting at a concert, a movie, a seminar, or a county fair.

Recreational Health

I hope you have a hobby. It could be an individual activity that helps you clear your head, like fishing, going for walks, or going for a run, or maybe you enjoy woodworking or sewing, where you get out of the norm and become creative. Some of you will enjoy a group exercise activity, such as a pickup game with friends, that builds relationships just because you took the time to spend together. This can be something you enjoy with others and add hours of pleasure to your life. In the dictionary, the word "fun" is a noun—a person, place, or thing. That disappoints me. I thought it would be a verb because when you're having fun, it's an activity.

I think hobbies should be fun—something that is amusing, something that's enjoyable; it makes you laugh when you do it, and you feel good inside. It's a natural stress reliever; it can get your mind off the dumb stuff in life. You'll find it has a way of recharging your batteries. You shouldn't have to go to a theme park to be amused in life. If you don't have a hobby, find one. Some suggestions include photography, boating, drawing, painting, and sculpting. Just Google the word hobby.

At this point, you should have a basic knowledge of our blueprint concept; it's still just a framework and a simple structure to design the kind of life you would think is worth living. Now it's time for action. Let's imagine for a moment, as you review the content of the previous paragraphs, you discover there are some changes you'd like to make in your life. I realize that change right now is still just in your mind, and if some form of anxiety follows the thought of making a change, I certainly understand that positive thoughts are often met with negative emotions. For example, you say to yourself, "I do need some good friends." Immediately, the feelings of social anxiety slow the excitement and the possibility of actually accomplishing that objective. What are your next steps? I'd start with what you enjoy doing. If you like cooking, there may be a class where those who have the same interests will be meeting to learn. How about art?

I imagine that someplace close to where you live, there is an art class, a museum, or a location where you could begin to interact with those who are interested in your interests. Make those phone calls now. Set down this book. Make a couple of phone calls to find out where they're meeting; set aside your schedule. Whoever is hosting that class is looking forward to meeting you and welcoming you with a sense of acceptance. They will ask you some questions in the hope of understanding where you are on your interest journey.

After that exchange, the interaction begins. You will learn something new, meet people, exchange emails and phone numbers, and begin the interaction we were created to enjoy. Trust me, a year from now, you won't be the same person; other people with common interests will enhance your life with content and substance, and you will be all the better for it.

13

WHAT SIGNIFICANCE DO DETAILED PLANS & ACTIONS HAVE?

We now embark on the realm of taking action and making plans. Having all the world's health tips but never lacing up your sneakers for a jog or knowing how to budget but never saving a penny, is like knowing the recipe for your favorite meal but never cooking it. Let's uncover the transformation that occurs when knowledge is put into action. Let's prepare ourselves to see how detailed planning and taking concrete steps can turn our aspirations into reality. It's not just about knowing what's good for us; it's about acting on that knowledge. So, let's dive into the heart of this matter.

A goal without a plan is just a wish. A coach once told me that knowledge plus action equals results. All the knowledge in the world, with no action implemented, still produces no results. All the actions with no knowledge being used still produce limited results; it's only when they both come together that you can produce optimal results.

Never confuse activity with productivity. Results define real success, and results are achieved by performance. When it comes to producing something, only results matter because that's what people will pay for, that is what they'll invest in, and that determines true value. Good intentions are nice, but results matter. As the old proverb puts it:

"The road to hell is paved with good intentions."

Let's say we wanted to build a house. The first thing we did was hire a contractor, agree on terms of construction, establish a scope of work, and endorse the new build contract on a Friday. On the following Monday, his first day at work, he talked about the house he would build. On his second and third days of work, he cleaned his tools. No house yet. On his fourth day of work, he organized the lumber. No house yet. On his fifth day of work, he looked at the blueprints. Still no house. On his sixth day of work, he surveyed the land. I'm looking for something that resembles a house.

On his seventh day of work, he talked again about the house that he would build. Wouldn't you, on the 8th day, start to wonder when he is going to build the house? RESULTS! Successful leaders concentrate on results. Certainly, the contractor busied himself; he used some energy and some effort, but I want a house. Real leadership develops winners who prove themselves with results, not whiners with reasons and excuses. Proverbs 13:4 says:

"The soul of the lazy man desires and has nothing, but the soul of the diligent shall be made rich."

Every person oversees building their own life. We are not born alone; there has to be someone outside of ourselves to help us with the birthing process, feed us, and change us. Over time, those who had some responsibility to provide care and help with our basic needs gave way to a desire to be more and more independent. And if we live life wisely, hopefully, we won't die alone but instead be surrounded by loved ones who were a part of our collection of relationships and partnerships that provided a sense of meaning and being. However, I pity the person who isolates themselves and behaves so independently that at the end of their time on earth, they are all by themselves. It's up to us to accept or reject the information we receive and the opportunities to build healthy relationships that last a lifetime.

So, if life hasn't turned out as you thought or planned, is there a real reason or just a somewhat empty excuse or justified obstacle? Think about this: how often do you say to yourself, "I should have, I would have, or I could have," but you didn't? Well, regardless of the reason, excuse, or obstacle, do you want to get past it and move forward?

Imagine two 15-inch monitors side by side, each playing a different version of your life. On one screen, there's the version of your life you thought you'd be living. On the other display, it's showing your real life. Is that hard to watch? Are you thinking somebody's living your life? What would be required to switch screens? Faith? Belief? Trust? Commitment? Whether you think it got robbed, stolen, hijacked, or just plain missed. It's never too late to start again.

God's will for your life is declared to be "good, perfect, and pleasing." Therefore, it stands to reason that it would be good for you, perfectly matching your talents and skills, and fully acceptable to live. Lasting pleasure and joy are a result of staying focused on your ultimate and individual purpose while pursuing the goals you set for your life to honor God. With your God-given gifts, talents, and abilities, you will find true fulfillment serving the people around you: your family, your friends, your associates, and your community. There is a great Anthony Robbins quote that emphasizes the importance of goal setting, as described in the next few paragraphs:

"The road to someday leads to a town of nowhere."

If you don't know where you're going, any road will take you there.

Now that you've seen the structure of The 4D Method, wouldn't it be wise to plan an attack on the areas where you know you need help to see true change? Are you ready to take the first step by understanding the process and discovering why those personal and professional goals are so important?

HOW CAN YOU APPLY THE PRINCIPLE THAT 'KNOWLEDGE PLUS ACTION EQUALS RESULTS' TO A CURRENT GOAL YOU ARE STRIVING TO ACHIEVE?

14

WHY WISHES DON'T WORK.
SMART GOALS DO.

Turning Plans into Action: Crafting SMART Goals

We are about to crack open the reason why mere wishes often fall short while SMART goals lead us to victory. It's like moving from the planning phase right into the heart of construction, where dreams start becoming a reality. We've seen how important it is to act on our plans, but now let's zoom in on crafting those plans with precision and clarity. As we step into the realm of goals, we're gearing up to transform those lofty wishes into an achievable reality. SMART GOALS are your toolkit for making dreams doable, guiding you from "I wish" to "I will."

The key difference between a wish and a goal lies in their substance and approach. A wish is a desire or hope for something to happen without a plan or the commitment to make it a reality. It's passive, relying on external forces or luck. On the other hand, a goal is a clearly defined objective that includes a plan of action and the intent to achieve it. Goals are active; they require commitment, effort, and a step-by-step approach to bring them to fruition. While wishes float in the realm of imagination, goals stand firm in the world of actionable steps and measurable progress. This distinction is crucial because wishes alone don't lead to achievements.

Supporting this concept, Proverbs 21:5 (NIV) states:

"The plans of the diligent lead to profit as surely as haste leads to poverty."

This verse emphasizes the importance of careful planning and diligent work in achieving one's goals, highlighting that mere wishes without diligent effort and planning are unlikely to result in success.

Years ago, I was introduced to a simple method for turning wishes into goals and goals into reality. It's called "SMART GOALS" and is built around an acronym for S.M.A.R.T., which helps establish practical, reasonable goals:

S | Specific: This is where your goal is both established and defined. It's about what you plan to achieve. For instance, if you're seeking more sales opportunities, the specifics may read like this: "I want five new accounts in the next 30 days, and I want the average contract amount to be $20,000." That is a specific goal.

M | Measured: Notice that when I specified my goal, I added numbers, amounts, and dates. Remember, your goals are your goals, and when you measure your goals, you determine how difficult or easy accomplishing them will be. Whether it's one new account with a price point of $5,000 or 30 new accounts with a price point of $2 million, with a date in place, you can establish the possibilities connected to your goals.

A | Achievable: This is where you consider all the possible obstacles to attaining your goal. Your demographics may change, the market could fluctuate, or you could lose a key member of your team. Taking the time to consider possible interruptions may cause you to adjust the specifics and measurements you're choosing to employ.

R | Realistic: Too often, we set unrealistic goals—they're either so low that they're not really goals or so high that they're unrealistic to reach. We've all seen the ads that run regularly with promises of better health and weight loss. I'm a skeptic. Losing

30 pounds in two weeks may sound tempting, but is it realistic and good for you long-term?

T | Timely: Every goal needs a clear deadline and a set start and end date to give it a sense of urgency. Without a deadline, motivation can wane because there's no pressing need to accomplish the goal. The letter 'T' in SMART can also stand for 'Test,' encouraging you to evaluate your goal's viability. This may entail discussing it with friends or sending out emails to see if your goal truly aligns with SMART criteria. Though this step might seem like it's part of measuring your goal, it actually serves as a crucial checkpoint to refine your strategy without penalty, should you initially fall short. I assure you that this isn't meant to offer an easy out. On the contrary, I encourage a relentless commitment to your goals. Recognizing the need for adjustment and persisting through challenges distinguishes true success from failure.

SMART goals convert nebulous wishes into concrete, achievable outcomes. They push us beyond wishful thinking and daydreaming into action, ensuring that our desires don't just remain desires but transform into realities through deliberate actions and perseverance.

DETAILING YOUR SMART GOALS JOURNEY

Below is the framework for SMART goal setting so you can input your current plan and expand as necessary. This process will help you define every aspect of your goals. It will also help you find the holes or empty spots that need work. You have a magnificent mind.

Let's embark on a journey of self-discovery and achievement using the SMART goals framework.

Personal and Professional Aspirations

S (Specific): Clearly define what success looks like in your personal and professional life.

M (Measurable): Set quantifiable indicators for progress.

A (Achievable): Ensure your goals are within reach given your current resources and constraints.

R (Realistic): Your aspirations should stretch your capabilities but remain possible.

T (Timely): Assign a deadline to each goal to foster urgency and commitment.

M.E.C. Health Goals

- **S (Specific)**: Pinpoint the exact skills or knowledge you aim to acquire for Mental health.

- **M (Measurable)**: Outline specific emotional states you wish to experience more frequently for Emotional health.

- **A (Achievable)**: Set practical challenges for your intellect to overcome for Cognitive health.

- **R (Realistic)**: Ensure each goal is achievable within a realistic timeframe.

- **T (Timely)**: Set specific timelines for achieving each health goal.

Physical Health Objectives

- **S (Specific)**: Detail the type, frequency, and intensity of exercise, nutrition plans, and maintenance practices.

- **M (Measurable)**: Establish benchmarks for tracking progress in physical activities, dietary habits, and self-care routines.

- **A (Achievable)**: Make sure the health objectives are attainable, given your current physical condition and lifestyle.

- **R (Realistic)**: Your health goals should be sensible and practically achievable.

- **T (Timely)**: Determine deadlines for achieving each physical health goal.

Financial and Work Growth

- **S (Specific)**: Define exactly how much value (in terms of revenue, savings, etc.) you aim to generate through Earning, Consuming, Saving, Investing, and Giving.

- **M (Measurable)**: Quantify your financial goals to track progress effectively.

- **A (Achievable)**: Choose financial targets that are ambitious yet attainable.

- **R (Realistic)**: Ensure they align with your overall financial plan and reality.

- **T (Timely)**: Establish deadlines for each financial milestone to maintain momentum.

Relational Well-being

- **S (Specific)**: Specify the practices for Divine Connection, the number of Social Engagements, and Recreational activities for joy.

- **M (Measurable)**: Establish clear criteria for measuring relational health improvements.

- **A (Achievable)**: Set relationship goals that are possible and meaningful.

- **R (Realistic)**: Ensure these goals are sensible and can be integrated into your daily life.

- **T (Timely)**: Apply timeframes to achieving relational milestones to ensure progress.

Daily Affirmations and Discipline

- **S (Specific)**: Write down clear affirming statements and a disciplined plan for achieving goals.

- **M (Measurable)**: Include measurable criteria to assess the impact of affirmations and discipline on your progress.

- **A (Achievable)**: Ensure the affirmations and discipline practices are feasible.

- **R (Realistic)**: Affirmations and discipline practices should be aligned with your overall objectives.

- **T (Timely)**: Set regular intervals for reviewing and adjusting your affirmations and discipline practices to stay on track.

Here's a sample SMART goal for daily exercise.

Specific: I enjoy doing a 30-minute workout every morning.

Measurable: I track my workouts using a fitness app to ensure I complete 30 minutes each day. I love keeping my commitment to myself.

Achievable: I am confident scheduling my workouts first thing in the morning, ensuring no other commitments can interfere.

Realistic: Considering my current fitness level and daily schedule, a 30-minute workout is challenging but doable.

Timely: Following this routine for the next 30 days and reassessing my progress at the end of this period is rewarding.

AFFIRMING GOAL CARDS

To help you get the most out of your SMART GOALS, write your goals on index cards. These are known as affirming goal cards to help you stay on track.

For the most retention, read these cards first thing in the morning and right before bed daily. Also, write some of the I AM foundational truth statements from chapter six into your affirming goal cards. Lastly, when writing these cards, remember to write positive present tense statements.

Here's an example of an Affirming Goal Card statement:

"I AM committed to improving my health and vitality by exercising for 30 minutes every morning. Each day, I grow stronger and more energized."

Integrating the SMART goals framework into each aspect of your life paves the way for a balanced, fulfilling journey. Visualize your progress, step by step, fueled by faith and determination towards success.

Be disciplined in all things. Make a plan and stick to it and adjust when necessary to get better results.

Remember, "I AM" is in me!

I was regretting the past and fearing the future.
Suddenly my Lord was speaking,
My name is I AM.

He paused, I waited. He continued.
When you live in the past
with its mistakes and regrets, it's hard.
I AM not there.
My name is not I WAS.

When you live in the future
With its problems and fears, it's hard.
I AM not there.
My name is not I WILL BE.

When you live in this moment,
It is not hard.
I AM here.

My name is I AM.

—Helen Mallicoat

DO YOU HAVE THE POWER TO TRANSFORM YOUR LIFE?

Evolving from the nuts and bolts of SMART goals to something more profound—the incredible journey of transforming your life. Let's make it personal and ask yourself, "Do I have the power to transform my life?"

Tapping into that amazing inner strength we all have is not just about setting goals; it's about changing from the inside out. We'll explore how your mind, faith, and positivity can become your most powerful allies. Get ready to see how you, yes, you, can become the architect of your destiny.

Diving into the essence of transformation, let's acknowledge the unassuming powerhouse within us all: the human brain. The human brain may not be attractive to look at, but every person should be fascinated and astounded by the way it works. It is the information station for our thoughts and decisions, our memories and emotions, all of our motor functions, our balance and coordination, the perception of various sensations (including pain), and automatic behaviors such as breathing, heart rate, sleep, temperature control, speech, and language functions. You are a walking miracle.

Neuroscience experts have studied the brain for years with many great discoveries, and yet there's so much we still don't know. What we do know is that positive impressions, whether they are audible or visible, can have a positive effect on our outlook and point of view. For instance, research shows that listening to uplifting music or viewing serene nature scenes can significantly boost mood and outlook, demonstrating the brain's remarkable responsiveness to positive inputs. This phenomenon underscores the potential for shaping our perspective and emotional well-being through carefully chosen experiences.

From a biblical perspective, faith in God and a belief that He is good and has a good plan for our lives have been catalysts for true and lasting change for many people. Biblical affirmations are one of many ways to influence the path and course of change in our lives.

Bible verses that declare truth, when memorized, can impact the way we act and behave. Something positive that's memorized can be attached to the subconscious, temporarily hidden in the recesses of your mind. A recall brings the truth to light, and in a time of need, it's available for action.

Years ago, I memorized James 1:19-20. It reads:

> *"Let every person be quick to hear, slow to speak, slow to anger, for the anger of man does not produce the righteousness of God."*

That truth became a part of my subconscious mind, and in a future disappointing and unfortunate situation, when I was feeling heated and anger started to rise within me, that Bible verse came to mind. Rather than reacting, I responded. I thought about my words and chose not to become angry. Recognizing that the fruit of my anger would only lead to greater disappointment in the very circumstances I was facing, I experienced victory over my emotions. What could have been a more dramatic conflict became an opportunity to resolve a misunderstanding. I behaved like the man I wanted to be rather than the man I was—a prime example of how a simple Bible verse fuels personal transformation.

As we delve into the essence of "The Power to Transform Your Life," it becomes clear that the journey of self-transformation is intricately linked to the choices we make every day. These choices, whether seemingly trivial or profoundly significant, lay the foundation for our future.

Your life is a collection of your choices—some good, some bad, some wise, some foolish, some great, and some dumb. The problem with choices is that we won't know their fruit until after they've been made. It would be wise to arrest our choices while they are still in a thought position before they become decisions. They can be checked, analyzed, and scrutinized with the goal of making the best choice.

Ralph Waldo Emerson said: "Sow a thought, and you reap an action; sow an act, and you reap a habit; sow a habit, you reap a character; sow a character, and you reap a destiny." Our destiny and all personal transformations are tied directly to and start with our thoughts.

Do you remember getting your first driver's license and the big test? While learning to drive, you memorize the fundamentals. Your hands belonged in the 10 and 2 positions; you practiced checking your rear-view mirror every six seconds; you knew before you left the curb you would have to adjust your seat and your seat belt, and you would never think of turning without using your signals. Your conscious mind was engaged, and you were very aware of your every move and gesture. That was years ago. Today, you don't have to give conscious thought to any of your driving. You travel with your subconscious connections memorized.

You still do all of the fundamentals; you just don't have to think of them. You are naturally good at driving. The same thing can happen with positive affirmations. Index cards can be used in the beginning for practice and memorization. Write down those key verses, those positive statements, and those hopeful aspirations. Recite them, record them, recall them, and commit them to memory. When you need them, they will be right there, at the forefront of your mind. It's a can-do attitude.

Philippians 4:13 is another memorized verse that resonates well with me and comes in handy.

"I can do all things through Christ who strengthens me."

As a follower of Christ, I have found that during times of growth and transformation, I can tap into greater hope by trusting someone greater than myself for my positive affirmations. Notice that I can do all things through Christ; that's where I get my strength.

I would now like to challenge you to find your own verses, quotes, and the truths that matter most to you. Write them down and start memorizing.

You do have the power to change. Bad habits can be broken, and good habits can be established. Consider everything you have learned in your lifetime:

- The books you have read.

- The information you have consumed.

- The sheer volume of all that content.

How much have you forgotten? Our brain uses what it needs and stores away ideas that are not needed. That is both a good and a bad thing. It's good to forget our past pain and all the events that led to negative emotions and trauma. However, the brain can relearn anything and, to its advantage, learn so much more.

Just like riding a bike, once you've learned something, your brain retains the skill, even if you haven't practiced it in a long time. A few attempts, and you're right back in the swing of things. Unlike muscles, which can weaken if not used, your brain maintains its abilities but needs engagement to stay sharp. Actively feeding positive and useful information not only preserves but also enhances your capabilities.

Leaving the intricate workings of the mind behind, let's address one of the greatest barriers to personal growth: the comfort zone. This snug and familiar territory, while offering a sense of security, often acts as a silent impediment to growth and transformation—inadvertently holding us back from reaching our full potential.

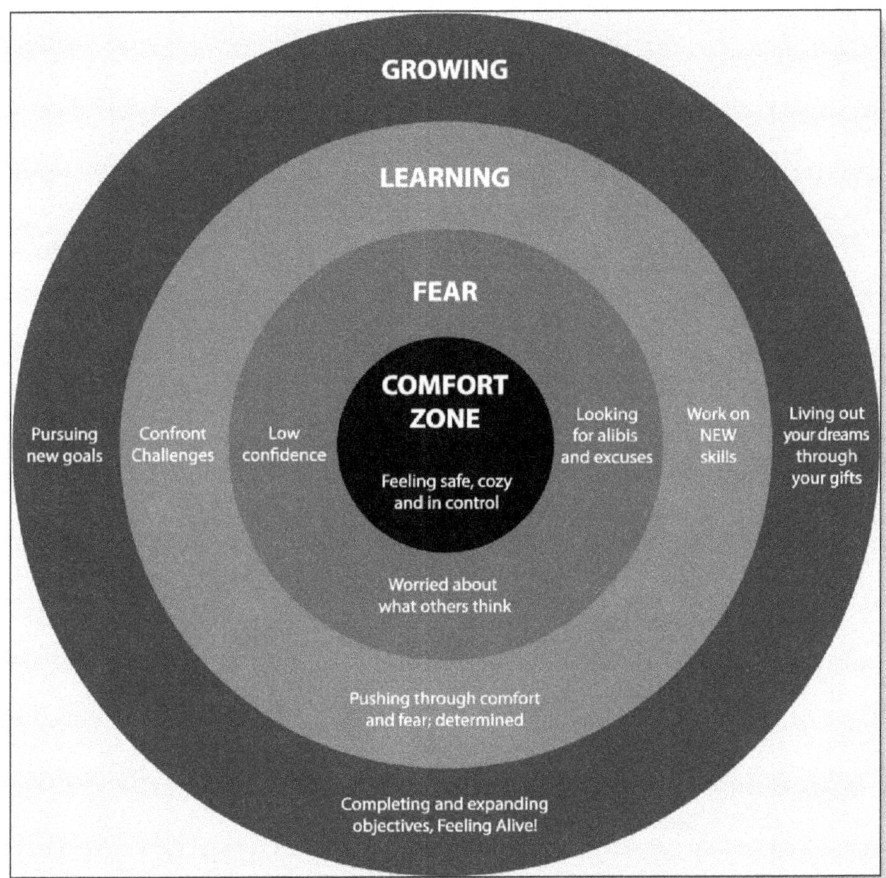

Expanding our Comfort Zone

Comfort zone? We use the word to describe a place or space that's almost utopian. The dictionary defines it as "a place or situation where one feels safe or at ease without stress." So, we find a comfortable sofa to sit on so we can enjoy our comfort food, surrounded by creature comforts, in a room with a comfortable temperature, around the folks we feel most comfortable with. And that's where we want to stay forever.

Therein lies the problem: comfort is safe, and our safe space is risk-free. Proverbs 22:13 declares: "There is a lion outside; I will be killed in the streets!" Lions didn't roam freely. This was an unjustified fear, and yet a lazy person will use any excuse to stay indoors in their place of comfort.

Sadly, fear will keep us from meeting new friends, traveling, speaking up, or doing anything different. But it's a choice. Some fears become so debilitating that we become housebound, and our lives become a mere shadow of our true existence.

It's interesting that so much marketing and selling is fixated on convincing people of their next "need." Convenience is what is sold, and it has everything to do with seeking more comfort.

Convenience and comfort are the enemies of transformation. Your conviction to change things usually parallels your frustration with the status quo.

Is it time? You've gotten this far in the book because, on some level, you are hungry to transform your life. You want an action plan to get out of the routine that has become a rut that you're stuck in. Now is the time; you are the person; this is the day, and all you needed was this simple nudge to take the next step.

In elementary school, we would often be dared to do something. Some crazy, foolish behavior flowed out of a dare. But what we are asking you to do is not crazy or foolish. It's wise, prudent, smart, and worth taking the next step.

So, I dare you—no, I double-dog dare you—to take the risk to transform your life in the image of Christ.

AS YOU CONSIDER STEPPING OUT OF
YOUR COMFORT ZONE, WHAT ACTION
CAN YOU TAKE THIS WEEK TO MOVE
CLOSER TO THE LIFE TRANSFORMATION
YOU DESIRE?

16

DO WE CHOOSE OUR PERSONALITY?

Having delved into SMART goals and the journey of self-transformation, we've explored the motivations behind our thoughts, how God perceives us, the milestones we've reached, and how to chart a path for improvement. Now, let's prepare our minds to examine the personalities we embody and the choices that shape them.

We live in an age of political correctness, where the risk of being "canceled" has caused a pendulum to swing in the opposite direction. For years, we enjoyed the freedom to express opinions based on observation and discernment. The word "stereotypical" isn't used as much anymore; it refers to a widely held but fixed and oversimplified image or idea of a particular type of person or thing.

For example, suggesting that boys aren't as good at following instructions or are less attentive than girls or that girls sometimes sulk too long over minor issues might be met with harsh judgment today. However, we must admit that certain key characteristics and personality traits are indeed common to all humankind.

We all possess traits from each of the profiles below, resembling four pieces of a pie. Many factors influence our unique style or personality. There is no right or wrong personality; every piece of the pie is good. We should be aware of ourselves—our own flavor and fashion. Understanding these profiles helps us see how we fit more perfectly into the mosaic of the world.

As you read through the next few pages, don't be surprised if you recognize some of these profiles as actual people you know. You might even discover aspects of yourself. Your professional and personal environments, as well as the influences that surround you, can cause adjustments in your personality profile. Remember, people change. If you notice something about yourself that isn't flattering, there's still hope; transformation and change are ongoing processes. There's an opportunity for growth in everyone. You may find that you identify with some aspects of one profile and more of another. Let's take a look.

IF YOU SEE A TRAIT IN YOURSELF THAT YOU'RE NOT PARTICULARLY FOND OF, WHAT STEPS CAN YOU TAKE TO BEGIN TRANSFORMING IT INTO THE PERSONALITY YOU ASPIRE TO EMBODY?

WHY A COMPILATION OF PERSONALITY PROFILES HELPS

Spending time to understand ourselves can be quite insightful, and spending time to understand the people around us will help us become a superior communicator.

The following four personality profiles can help explain why we are naturally drawn to some people while we might avoid others. While everyone possesses elements of each type, we all have strengths in certain areas. The best communicators in the world know how to understand other people's points of view and talk to them on their own terms.

Let's explore these four personality types.

1. **The Lions** (Aggressive): Lions are powerful and commanding, naturally taking charge and leading with authority. They are bold and fearless, always ready to pounce on opportunities and overcome challenges.

2. **The Owls** (Analytical): Owls are wise and observant, meticulously analyzing situations before making decisions. They are known for their patience and ability to see the bigger picture while focusing on the details.

3. **The Monkeys** (Influential): The Monkeys are excited and charismatic, drawing attention with their charm and creativity. They thrive in social settings, spreading their ideas and influencing others with their enthusiasm.

4. **The Dolphins** (Supportive): Dolphins are gentle and nurturing and are nown for their strong sense of community and empathy. They excel at building relationships and maintaining harmony, always looking out for the well-being of others.

The Lions

Lions can be identified quickly—they include the lawyer or salesman and the consummate controller. Lions are dominant and driven. The color we use to define them is Ferrari red. They are a D on the DISC survey and a true alpha. They are disciplined, fairly formal, and well-dressed, though sometimes without a tie to prove they don't have to wear one. Lions are direct and very self-contained, and their appearance and attitude are all business—very functional and power-oriented. If you visit their office, you'll see they're very busy, efficient, and incredibly structured in their lifestyle. They love having priorities, tasks, and results. They're the type who will size you up quickly; they want to know your qualifications, track record, and value to the team. You must prove that your product or service brings great value to the table.

Lions hate to lose, fear losing control, are great delegators, like to dictate what needs to be done next, and will insert their opinion even when not asked. Highly productive, Lions support their ideas and conclusions with questions, which they ask only to appear interested or to qualify your value. When inviting them to participate in anything, introduce them to what your product or service does, when it will arrive, and how much it will cost. If you're going to do business with Lions, get documentation because they may tend to shift direction midstream. Their tone is typically forceful and has enough volume because they must be heard. Keywords they live by may include money, power, and control. When communicating with them, it's best to "get to the point." They're really turned off by indecision, chit-chat, and wasting time.

Don't be surprised by a Lion's almost rude behavior; when they tell you to "get out of the way," it's best you move. Lions are good at organizing, especially if they are in charge. They are improvers and will try to convince you that theirs is the best idea. They are always focused on the ROI of everything and will first consider the bottom line in most negotiations. They have a tough time listening because, of course, they already know the answer to everything. They are typically successful, at least financially; they thrive where recognition or competition is involved. Lions tend to drive and wear iconic symbols of brands that impress others; comparing themselves to others is a pastime. Their handshake is typically vise-grip strong; it's a display of confidence and authority, usually with a twist or a pull to show who's in charge. They'll work the room, looking for others like themselves or those who will make them look good if seen together. They are most often self-employed and excel at top jobs, such as CEO, attorney, pilot, or politician.

The Owls

Owls tend to be very analytical. They seem wise and patient, and their decisions are measured and analyzed. They are the letter C on a DISC survey; their color is green. They are slower-paced and disciplined; their appearance and attitude are more businesslike, conservative, and detail-oriented. They probably wear a tie even when they don't have to. An Owl's workspace is structured and organized, making it very functional; everything has a place and a space. You'll find them on research and development teams, filling accounting positions, and most engineers fall into this category. They are meticulously systematic and very self-disciplined. The task and its process are top priorities. If an Owl decides to partner with you, it's because of your experience and knowledge.

Owls love solving problems, and their greatest fear is the embarrassment of an error they should have seen. In stressful environments, they will typically withdraw or avoid contact or conversation. They're very accurate and live by principles and rationale. Vulcan—a term popularized by Star Trek—would be another word to describe their style. When an Owl purchases products, it needs to make sense—more logic than emotion—and they love to understand how things work. There is no place for fluff. Owls need evidence to convince them that your service or product really works. Their downfall is that they can be overly analytical and very hard to please; they can get depressed and feel lonely when not appreciated or valued.

Owls love the "why" of everything; they like charts and graphs, spreadsheets tickle them, and bracketed amounts bother them because they live in a world of exact numbers. They are turned off by pushy people, the lack of facts, anyone who's late, and people who are lazy. An Owl's tone is usually very soft and well-mannered, and they are polite to others. They will ask for information, and once received, don't be surprised if they want it verified. They can be anal at times in their research; they're often skeptical, so don't be surprised if they ask more questions than most. And please, do not use round numbers; be specific. Again, accuracy is an important part of the way they do life. Owls love to follow the rules. When you shake their hand, it will feel controlled; they are somewhat methodic, so don't expect a lot of emotion. They carry a briefcase and a portfolio, and if they're minimizing, they'll still have a manila folder with paper clips and Post-it notes, all color-coordinated.

The Monkeys

Monkeys are influencers. They are great at promoting anything. They are very expressive; in school, they were probably the class clown. On some personality color charts, they are blue, and in the DISC survey, they are yellow. They love conversation and people and are energetic, fast-paced, and somewhat undisciplined. They will naturally take charge when there's a game to be played or a joke to be told.

Monkeys communicate openly and directly. Their overall appearance is fashionable; they appreciate style. They are quickly organized and ready to lead an activity. Their workspace is stimulating and somewhat cluttered, but they are always approachable. Monkeys make good salespeople, entertainers, public speakers, and stand-up comedians. They're spontaneous and eager to please; they tend to build relationships quickly because they love interaction. They're interested in who you are, what you think, and what you know.

Monkeys fear public humiliation and the loss of prestige and position. Under pressure, they can be humorously sarcastic, hoping to be still heard. Recognition means a lot to them because they are interested in others; their interest often extends to understanding someone else's feelings, interests, and sense of purpose. When facilitating a decision, do your best to provide guarantees and assurances. They will be interested in opinions more than options. They will tend to be slow when closing a sale because they don't want to risk losing a relationship they would rather keep.

The potential downfall for Monkeys is that they tend to talk too much when they should be doing the job. To achieve their goals, they should focus more on follow-up and their organizational skills. Their tone is louder than most; it's their laugh you can hear from the other office. They speak more words per minute than most. If you spend time with a Monkey, expect to have fun; it will always be an adventure.

It's been said of the Monkey personality that they've never met a stranger, and they enjoy selling. Their personality typically makes them popular; they're the ones you want to take to the party. Monkeys believe they are great multitaskers, but they're not. They would rather be at the water cooler in conversation than sit behind their desk. They are quick to give out compliments, and flattery comes naturally, but their goal is to be liked more.

Like *Tigger* from *Winnie the Pooh*, they tend to walk with a slight bounce. They smile all the time, are outgoing, and love to think big picture and big vision, but the details need to be given to someone else. They are great storytellers. Monkeys communicate best with their hands. They don't mind taking risks; they're always looking forward and optimistic. Money motivates these people, and they love to cheer for the underdog.

The Dolphins

Picture a Dolphin—playful, kind, and attuned to the needs of others. They are known for their gentle nature and strong sense of community. Dolphins glide through life with a relaxed and free-spirited approach, enjoying deep conversations and meaningful connections. Once they trust you, they are open and non-threatening, always ready to offer support. Their style is casual and non-conforming, reflecting their easygoing personality. Dolphins often choose careers in nursing, counseling, teaching, or other nurturing roles. If you are trustworthy, friendly, and approachable, you might win a Dolphin's lifelong friendship. They move through life at a steady, easy pace, avoiding confrontation and preferring to maintain peace, even under pressure.

Dolphins are servant-minded at heart, valuing recognition and attention in their daily responsibilities. Often well-educated, their ideas and natural intuitions contribute significantly when they are part of a team. They seek to understand how any decision affects them personally, and they are particularly drawn to helping others who have experienced pain, trouble, or difficulty. Their voices are soft and gentle; they are good listeners, and, like Florence Nightingale—the pioneering nurse known for revolutionizing healthcare and tirelessly caring for the wounded—they endure others' hardships, believing it is their calling in life.

However, a Dolphin's gentle nature can also be a drawback. They can be overly sensitive and may struggle to set goals, but when they are part of a team, they give their all. They dislike pushy people, bullies, and conflict. Dolphins love kids and animals, are highly credible, and have a strong sense of faith. They are natural, with minimal use of makeup, and are very organized, great multitaskers, but tend to be indecisive, often failing to see the importance of strategy. Dolphins can be easily guilted into doing things they're not interested in and are not particularly money motivated. Dependable, patient, supportive, and nurturing, Dolphins also make great moms.

Now that you are familiar with the four personality profiles, which one do you identify with the most? Are you more of a Lion—a bold leader—or an Owl—a meticulous planner? Perhaps you are the charismatic and influential Monkey, or the empathetic and nurturing Dolphin. When you think of family and friends, which profiles do they align with most?

Each personality type has its own strengths. It's important to remember that we shouldn't rush to label any of these profiles as good or bad, positive or negative. No one is better than the other, so please refrain from doing that! The point of understanding these is to appreciate that we're all different—we all communicate differently, and that's a wonderful thing. The world needs all kinds of people: the compassionate nurse, the sharp salesman, the wise accountant, and the entertaining comedian. Everyone has a role to play, and there's a place for everyone.

We all have our strengths when it comes to how we communicate, and it's natural to want to be recognized for the things we do well rather than judged for our shortcomings. Knowing what you do well is key. For example, if you're a Lion, you might be great at taking charge, or if you're a Dolphin, you excel at building relationships. Whatever your strengths are, focus on them and use them to your advantage. By understanding and embracing your natural abilities, you can build stronger connections and navigate situations with more confidence.

However, it's also important to recognize where you might need to grow. Sometimes, our approach needs to be freshened up. By understanding your strengths and making small adjustments in how you communicate with others, you can prevent frustration and disappointment. These subtle changes, guided by an understanding of different personalities, really do make a difference in how well you connect with people.

Our communication tendencies aren't set in stone. All of us make adjustments to our personalities over time, and that's a good thing. Imagine how dull life would be if we all thought and communicated the same way. For example, I've lived in the same place for a long time, but I'm always making improvements. Sometimes, it's a full redecoration, and other times, it's just small changes that make the space feel fresh. Some of you may have moved, searching for that perfect place or at least a better fit. The same approach applies to how you interact with the four personality profiles. Keep making improvements, and if necessary, don't be afraid to make bigger changes that can transform your surroundings and help you live the life you want. That's what this book is here to help you understand: those subtle adjustments really do matter!

Knowing these personality types can help you connect with others on a deeper level. Instead of trying to change those around you to see your point of view, it's far more beneficial to adjust your approach based on their natural communication tendencies. For example, if you're a fast-talking Monkey working with an Owl who values precision, you'll need to slow down and provide the details they need to feel like you are really communicating with them. By doing so, you prevent the frustration that comes from unmet expectations and foster stronger, more harmonious relationships—whether in your personal life or at work.

No matter what dominant personality you are, everyone wants to be heard and understood; communication, therefore, becomes an art form. Knowing these different personality profiles will assist you in your attempt to connect. First, you must accept the differences of others; the attempt to change someone typically ends in futility. Second, it's important to adjust how we communicate. If you're a "Monkey" type salesperson looking to sell to a "Lion" type personality, they don't want to hear another colorful story about your last client; they probably want you to stop talking and give them the price. Your awareness of this fact enables you to be more in tune with some-one else's point of view and in sync with them as you communicate. If not, you'll experience unmet expectations, wondering why you didn't close the sale or secure that second date. Unmet expectations can lead to resentment, bitterness, and a sense of self-defeat.

Consider this: a person's perception is their reality, and taking the time to understand them will always be priceless. Allow people to be who they are, adjust your communication, and be aware of how your words are being received. It's worth noting that some sections in this book come with a warning label, maybe even a disclaimer: "The information you just discovered can be used for both good and bad purposes." Natural charm can be a powerful tool for persuasion and encouragement. However, using these insights in the wrong way can easily turn into manipulation, coercing people into things they may later regret. Every strength has the potential to become a weakness if not guided by pure intentions and kept under the control of the gift-giver, God.

John Maxwell explains well in "Ethics 101" that ethics cannot be categorized in our lives. People try to use one set of ethics for their professional life, another set for their spiritual life, and still another at home with their family. This gets them in trouble. Ethics is ethics, he explains. If we desire to be ethical, we live by one standard across the board. In other words, there are no such things as business ethics. When leaders find a standard of value to guide their lives, they can be ethical wherever they go. I believe the scriptures teach that one standard is The Golden Rule:

> *"Do unto others what you would have them
> do unto you" (Matthew 7:12).*

When personal convenience, getting results, winning, rationalizing our decisions, or revenge are more important to us than doing what's right, we will act unethically when the going gets tough.

HAVE YOU EVER FELT MISUNDERSTOOD BECAUSE OF YOUR PERSONALITY TRAITS? HOW CAN UNDERSTANDING DIFFERENT PERSONALITY PROFILES HELP YOU COMMUNICATE MORE EFFECTIVELY WITH OTHERS?

18
HOW WE VIEW OTHERS MATTERS

Let's dive into the heart of how we see the world and each other. It's all about perception—the magical tool that allows us to connect with people on a deeper level. Think of it like tuning your radio to your favorite station; when you adjust your perception, you start hearing the music of life more clearly.

Perception: The ability to see, hear, or become aware of something through the senses.

This definition highlights perception as our gateway to understanding the world around us. By refining our perception, we can better interpret the signals life sends our way, enhancing our interactions and deepening our connections with others.

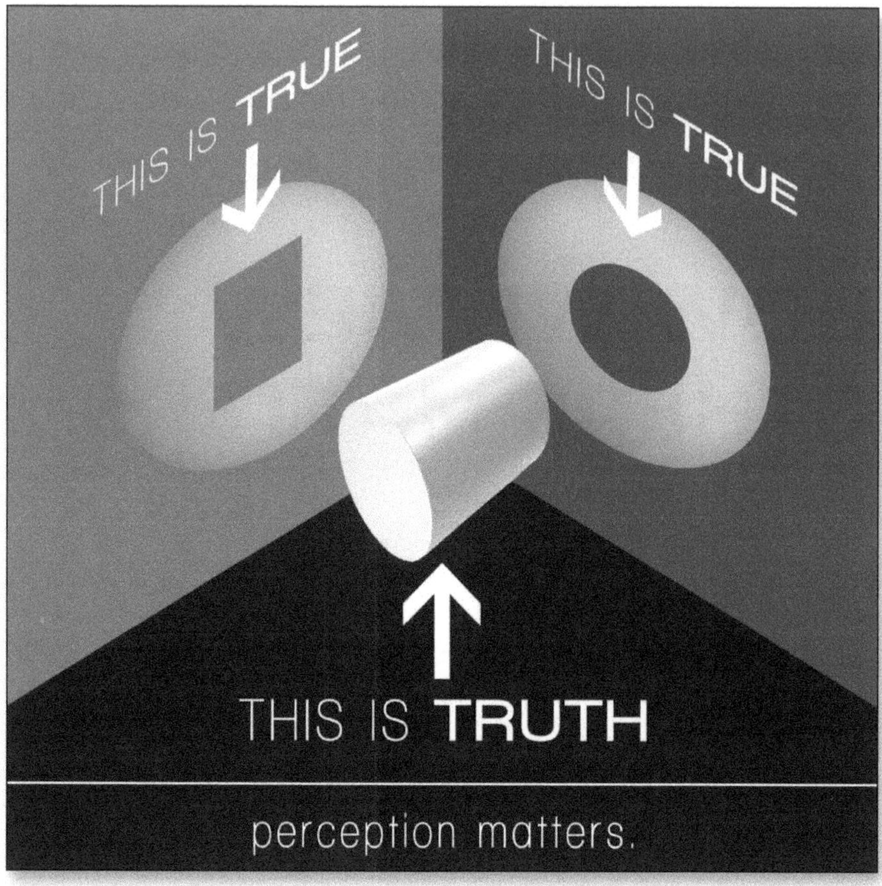

Have you ever wondered what it would take to better connect with the world around you, positively influence others, and make connections more naturally? If you closely examine your life, you may notice certain trends or patterns in how you view others. Reflecting on these patterns can help you identify the type of people you're hoping to connect with. While we can't control the environment we're born into, as we move through life, we can choose to adjust our perception of the people we connect with.

In the Dale Carnegie classic, *How to Win Friends and Influence People*, an important truth emerges thematically: Everyone's favorite subject is themselves. Your perception of others becomes a discovery tool that allows you to tune in, listen more attentively, observe more compassionately, and pay attention to the details of their personalities. Everyone wants to be understood; your perception becomes your ability to know, and your newly acquired knowledge leads to understanding.

This book began with the desire to help you know yourself—to clear the fog in your mirror of reflection and provide you with a view that can assist in making necessary changes on the path to a better you.

The phrase "know thyself" is often attributed to Sigmund Freud. However, these words were inscribed almost as a warning in the pronaos of the Temple of Apollo at Delphi. Plato, who communicated this phrase through his dialogues, emphasized the importance of looking inward before making decisions or taking steps forward. How you view others is an outpouring of how you view yourself.

It's tragic that so many still find themselves helpless when it comes to self-knowledge. Our society continues to act without first reflecting, then blames others for its failures, and ultimately behaves without real integrity. Self-knowledge and self-awareness are the essence of human maturity and foster a more compassionate and understanding view of others. Personal development is your greatest responsibility, a task to which you should devote time, insight, and effort.

Jesus urged his disciples to remove the log from their own eyes before attempting to remove the speck from someone else's eye.

"And why worry about a speck in your friend's eye[a] when you have a log in your own? 4 How can you think of saying to your friend,[b] 'Let me help you get rid of that speck in your eye,' when you can't see past the log in your eye? 5 Hypocrite! First, get rid of the log in your own eye; then, you will see well enough to deal with the speck in your friend's eye."
Matthew 7:3-5 (NLT)

UNDERSTANDING THE IDEA THAT
EVERYONE'S FAVORITE SUBJECT IS
THEMSELVES, HOW CAN YOU USE
THIS KNOWLEDGE TO ENHANCE YOUR
INTERACTIONS AND DEEPEN YOUR
CONNECTIONS WITH OTHERS?

WHAT ABOUT JUDGING OURSELVES AND OTHERS?

"Judge not lest you be judged."

Jesus spoke those words, which are recorded for us in Matthew's Gospel, Chapter 7:1.

The word for "judge" in the original language is "KRINO," which means to separate, to put under, to pick out, to select, to choose, or to hold an opinion. It's also used in a court of law to punish or pass a sentence. We might use the word "condemn." I can't, nor should I, condemn anyone because, with God, there is always a second chance—and a third, and a fourth. Until we are dead, there is always an opportunity for a "do-over," a chance to change. This concept of second chances should fill you with hope and reassurance.

However, there is another word for "judge" in the Bible: "DIAKRI-NO," meaning to discern, to scrutinize, or to examine. If I go to a restaurant and order a burger, and the waitress comes back with a chicken sandwich, and I inform her, "You got the order wrong,"

I'd be dumbfounded if she replied, "Judge not lest you be judged." You see, I'm not condemning her behavior by pointing out that she brought me the wrong order; I'm simply correcting it. That is the kind of judgment that is helpful and necessary in life. It's the kind of judgment that assists us in making good choices.

The Bible teaches that God is jealous for us, not of us. He wants our choices to result in the best life possible. It's the same way we, as parents, feel about our children; we are jealous for them, not of them. So, when we judge their choice in picking a school or the person they will date, our participation in providing an opinion is dedicated to helping them make the best choice—wise decisions.

It's very important to understand the difference as we move forward into the next chapters. I want you to judge (DIAKRINO) your life! I want you to examine it, to pick it apart, with a goal. Discover the places where you, deep inside your being, know it's high time you made some adjustments.

1 Corinthians 11:31:

> *"For if we would (DIAKRINO) discern, examine ourselves, we should not be (KRINO) condemned."*

I've often tried to be a harsh judge of myself and a compassionate discerner of others. Remember, as you discern someone else's life, it's not to judge or condemn; it's to understand them.

REFLECTING ON THE DUAL MEANINGS OF "JUDGE" IN THE BIBLE, HOW CAN YOU APPLY THE PRINCIPLE OF DISCERNMENT (DIAKRINO) IN YOUR DAILY LIFE TO HELP YOU MAKE MORE INFORMED AND COMPASSIONATE DECISIONS?

20

HOW TO UNDERSTAND SOCIETY IN FOUR CATEGORIES

Warning: What you're about to read next may seem harsh, hard, condescending, or even personally convicting, so buckle up. It could get bumpy.

The next phase of understanding why we judge ourselves and others begins with an exploration of four distinct attributes of society. I first learned these concepts many years ago from one of my first business mentors, who shared these concepts with me.

Understanding these categories, from the unmovable to the unstoppable, opens up a world of insights into how we interact with the people around us. It's like having a map that shows us why we click with some and clash with others and how we can navigate our social world more smoothly.

By examining each group's traits, we'll see not only where we might fit but also how we can adjust our sails to catch the winds of better relationships and personal growth. Whether we're looking to deepen our connections or get a clearer picture of the social landscape, this promises to shed light on the path to better understanding others and ourselves.

Anytime someone creates a way to understand society through classifications, there are obviously some generalities that allow us to form the categories. That being said, if you spend the time really understanding the attributes of each category, it will not only be personally convicting but will also allow you to discern with greater accuracy the attributes of the people you are associating with.

Being able to recognize variations in these attributes will also help you manage your time more effectively. So often, we don't realize how much time we waste with the wrong people when all the clues are right in front of us. No matter what your motivation may be for building a relationship, understanding where the other person is coming from and how they see the world is paramount.

The four categories

1. Unmotivatable

2. Motivatable

3. Self-motivated

4. Motivator

Unmotivatable

This section of society wants direction and will only put minimal effort into thinking. Sadly, this group will never win because they never make an attempt. Their goal in life is to ensure that no one else succeeds either.

This person is very negative, always on the defensive, self-centered, and inconsiderate. They'll pick a fight and argue about almost everything. They're critical, and they love to find faults in others. They have a hard time admitting their own mistakes. They're not real team players and have trouble understanding others or seeing any value in their ideas. They're skeptical and suspicious of everyone else's motives. They enjoy gossiping and talking negatively about their jobs and bosses. They're not good listeners, and they spend most of their time trying to convince people of their strengths instead of developing them.

Motivatable

These are the people who tell themselves they hope they can win, but what they really do is wish they could win. They want to avoid problems, keep their heads down, follow the crowd, and live a very safe life. They want guarantees in life and prefer to live one day at a time.

They're very self-conscious, lack confidence in what they do, and tend to be indecisive. Their energy level is low, and they lack drive and passion. Their free time is spent sharing their problems with anyone who will listen. They have a poor self-image and yet crave the approval of others. They tend to lie to themselves, are critical of themselves, and are extremely sensitive to criticism. They are worrywarts, view risk as an invitation for failure, and are quick to blame others for their lot in life. They tend not to learn from their mistakes but instead repeat them.

Self-motivated

These people put a lot of thought into everything they do. They often win, but it requires a lot of effort. They will take calculated risks and enjoy solving problems.

In most cases, they behave responsibly. They have a good self-image and are confident in what they do. They maintain good boundaries and limit their problem-sharing to a small number of people. They do their best to understand and be tolerant of others. They typically have a higher energy level, drive, passion, and a positive attitude.

They are good listeners and active participants on any team. They tend to be flexible and accept the ideas of others. They are comfortable in their own skin and allow others to be the same. They are highly interested in other people and their life experiences. They truly believe that experience is the best teacher.

Motivator

This group is made up of those who light the fire under other people to take action and get things done. They intend to win and seek solutions to problems. They love to take risks, and although they make a lot of mistakes, they usually succeed because they're consistently seeking to improve themselves. They live by the mandate: if at first you don't succeed, try, try, try again. They are fully aware that you will miss 100% of the shots you never take.

These are the people who wake up energized. They have extremely high energy levels and a positive self-image. Criticism from others, they believe, is simply a tool to make the necessary adjustments in their lives for improvement. They're good communicators and powerful persuaders. They're very self-confident and goal oriented.

Motivators are willing to admit that they made a mistake, learn from it, and move on. They are humble and quick to give approval and recognition to others who deserve it. They understand and accept the motivation of others. They are self-starting and self-motivated. They live in the light of the truth and are very self-aware. They know their strengths, but they are also aware of their weaknesses.

Did you see parts of yourself in what we just reviewed? Chances are, you did. Some of the things you just read puffed you up just enough to make you feel good about yourself. However, some of what you read may have caused you to feel that slight palpitation of panic. You know it's not the best side of you, and yet it comes out. Sometimes, when you least expect it, here comes that characteristic that you wish you had more control over. The good news is that none of these characteristics are necessarily hardwired, and they are subject to change. You are the agent of change, personally and practically.

In James 1:23, we read:

"Anyone who listens to the word but does not do what it says is like someone who looks at his face in a mirror and, after looking at himself, goes away and immediately forgets what he looks like."

I don't know too many people who get up in the morning, look at their faces in the mirror, and don't see the need for change. Men shave, comb their hair, and wash their faces; women put on makeup and do their hair. There is always a need for change. James is not being facetious; at the same time, it would be silly or absurd to look in the mirror in the morning, see the need for change, and do nothing about it. In the same way, one of the objectives of this book is to show that a change should be made, can be made, and that you are the one to make the change.

We must be willing to replace our bad habits with new ones, and that starts with getting out of our comfort zone, as we talked about earlier. We used to call them couch potatoes; they were people who liked to stay in their PJs with a bowl of sugary cereal in their lap, unshaven, binge-watching their favorite show, and unwilling to move because they were just so comfortable.

Now, if they are 40 years old, and that sofa is in the basement of their parents' house, and they don't have a job and lack the motivation to get one, you may be scratching your head, wondering, "How is that comfortable?" Reading what was just written, you're in one of two positions: you're either chuckling with embarrassment for the person on that sofa, or you are that person, and it is imperative—it is time to change.

RECOGNIZING TRAITS FROM EACH CATEGORY THAT RESONATE WITH YOU, WHICH ATTRIBUTES WOULD YOU LIKE TO DEVELOP FURTHER TO ENHANCE YOUR RELATIONSHIPS AND EFFECTIVENESS IN YOUR COMMUNITY OR WORKPLACE?

Three

DECIDE & DECLARE

In any moment of decision, the best thing you can do is the right thing. The worst thing you can do is nothing.
—Theodore Roosevelt

21

HOW TO IMPLEMENT REVEALED INFORMATION TO IMPROVE RELATIONSHIPS

The term "revelation" often refers to the discovery of a surprising or remarkable quality in someone or something. Gaining such a revelation about a person typically comes from investing time, showing genuine interest, and engaging thoughtfully with them.

Once you uncover these meaningful insights, you can use this knowledge in various ways, such as sharpening your perception. This involves enhancing your ability to notice and understand the deeper, sometimes hidden aspects of situations or individuals. It's about becoming more aware so that you can more effectively identify important truths or insights.

For example, developing Situational Intelligence (SI) and Situational Awareness (SA) is important and helpful.

(SI) Situational Intelligence

Anticipation: Identifying potential challenges and dynamics within a situation before they unfold.

Making informed decisions by synthesizing a variety of information.

Action: Responding effectively based on a comprehensive understanding of the situation.

SI not only improves the ability to perceive the immediate environment, but also foresee changes, and respond knowledgeably and appropriately.

(SA) Situational Awareness

This is understood through three ascending levels.

1. **Perception of the elements in the environment:** Noticing and recognizing what is happening around you.

2. **Comprehension of the situation:** Understanding the significance of the environmental elements and their implications.

3. **Projection of future status:** Anticipating potential future events based on current understanding.

Combining SI and SA gives people the tools they need to see ahead, understand, and respond well to tricky situations. This helps them make smarter choices and interact better with others and their surroundings.

If you're familiar with the *Iron Man* movie series, Tony Stark is the perfect example of someone who has amazing situational awareness. When he climbs into his specially made artificial intelligence body armor, with the push of a button, his face is illuminated with an amazing array of informative data points. Everything he needs to know is available with just a slight shift of his eyes, including the body temperature of the person he's talking to, whether there are adversarial weapons in the room, his heart rate, external threats, who might be hiding in the other room, and so on.

Talk about reading a room! Wouldn't it be to our advantage if, in fact, we knew if the person we were meeting with felt rushed, had a bad morning, was struggling with some addictive behavior, or was going through a divorce?

With the insights gained from understanding situational Intelligence (SI) and situational awareness (SA), we're better equipped to navigate the complexities of human relationships. Let's explore the realm of empathy and genuine connection, where caring deeply for others and desiring stronger bonds become our focus.

If we lack empathy, we really don't care. But if we genuinely care about other people and want to build better relationships, we will mentally take note of this desire and be more intentionally compassionate and sympathetic toward others.

We will be more aware through communication, asking questions, being genuinely interested in learning more about the people around us, and paying attention to our environments. Once we understand the people around us and their general personalities and are situationally intelligent and aware, we can communicate in a way that the people around us will gladly receive information from us because we now have a better understanding of the current needs in the conversation. This is how we relate to others and build genuine relationships.

When talking about awareness, it's noteworthy that Jesus, as he was talking to his disciples, changed up two very similar sentences with the adjustment of just one word. In Matthew 4:24, Jesus told the disciples to "take heed **what** they hear." This has everything to do with content. It implies listening to what is true and not what is false, not giving heed to gossip or slander, but instead hearing the words that benefit and bless.

However, in Luke 8:18, again, Jesus speaks to his disciples and says, "Take heed **how** you hear." Notice the subtle difference: on one occasion, he emphasizes **what** they hear, and on another occasion, he emphasizes **how** they hear. The word **"what"** has everything to do with content, and **"how"** has everything to do with perception.

We tend to size people up quickly when we meet them; statistically speaking, it's said that our words only account for 7% of what someone hears. Body language is higher, of course, at 38%, and tone of voice accounts for even more—closer to 55%. Those who study body language have a lot to say about tuning in to someone's mannerisms as they communicate, allowing the listener to adjust what's being said to how it's being said. Situational awareness and situational Intelligence are just that. It's a conscious effort to truly tune in when listening on every occasion.

I want to give you a simple tool to help you better communicate. This tool applies to both SA and SI.

Before I connect with anyone, I think of the word *LISTEN*. Remember this acronym:

- **L**: Look around and observe the environment.

- **I**: Investigate by asking follow-up questions.

- **S**: Use all your senses to perceive cues.

- **T**: Talk less and listen more.

- **E**: Engage in genuine communication.

- **N**: Take note of the conversation's significant details.

L: Look. Whatever the environment, I look around. Are there pictures on the wall that connect me to the person I'm meeting with or talking to? I look to see if the person is out of breath; maybe they are in a rush, and I'm unknowingly interrupting something. Is there a trinket on their desk that gives me a clue about their hobbies or interests, like a model car, a model plane, or a baseball? I look around.

I: Investigate. Just like a reporter asking the kind of questions that don't feel intrusive but are simple follow-ups to what I already know;

for instance, if I've already asked, "Are you married?" a follow-up might be, "Do you have any kids?" Next, "What are their ages?" If I see a trophy fish on the wall, I want to know the occasion it was caught, as well as the friends he was with on the boat. Genuine interest goes a long way in showing that you care.

S: Senses. I'm reinforcing the need to use all my senses. What do I see, what do I hear, and what did I feel when I shook their hand? If their palms were sweaty, that's a good indication that they might be nervous. It's my opportunity to put them at ease. If it's one of those strong, hurt handshakes, I'll typically make a lighthearted comment and find out where they have a gym membership. You get the idea.

T: Talk less, slow down. I need to listen more than I talk. Those who study sales techniques suggest that those representing a product should speak 30% of the time and listen 70% of the time. If you talk more than you listen, it's an indication that you care more about being known than knowing more about the person you're connecting with.

E: Engage. At some point in the dialogue, you should feel that real communication is happening beyond just exchanging facts, knowledge, or why your product is better than your competitors. You should feel the exchange of engagement; you're aware of the needs, you understand the opportunity, and you're building the relationship.

N: Notable. This is your opportunity to take note of the conversation and literally note some standout quality—something unique about the conversation's content that will not be easily forgotten. If the person you were talking to were transparent enough to tell you something personal about their health or a struggle they're going through, I would go so far as to put a follow-up call on my calendar, show a little compassion, and see how they're doing. When you take the time to care and display that care authentically and genuinely, the dividends from what was going to be just a simple conversation will last for years to come. I believe it's how strangers become friends.

That is a simple way to put SA and SI into your communication skills.

James 1:19 says:

> *"My dear brothers and sisters, take note of this: Everyone should be quick to listen, slow to speak, and slow to become angry."*

How many of us have regrets after a conversation is over, replaying what we should have said and being disappointed about what we didn't say? Trying to be quick-witted and clever, our words may have fallen flat.

For example, I've attended meetings and observed people listening while others spoke. Those who didn't think before they spoke were less impactful, while those who did think about what they were going to say were understood because of the clarity and substance of the content they conveyed.

But I also noticed that some people, when they speak, are unaware that those who are listening don't care to pay attention because they feel as though they won't miss anything due to a lack of substance.

It's always great to be prepared and aware of how people are responding to your communication.

CONSIDERING YOUR CURRENT RELATIONSHIPS, HOW MIGHT IMPROVING YOUR SITUATIONAL INTELLIGENCE (SI) AND SITUATIONAL AWARENESS (SA) ENHANCE YOUR INTERACTIONS AND UNDERSTANDING OF OTHERS?

22

DO WE ALL GO THROUGH STAGES OF LEARNING?

Absolutely, we do! Let's move towards understanding our journey of competence and learning as we delve into the four distinct stages of learning that each of us experiences. Starting from unconscious incompetence, where we blissfully ignore our lack of skill, to the ultimate goal of unconscious competence—performing tasks with effortless expertise—the four stages of learning guide us through this universal process of growth and discovery.

The Four Stages of Learning

1. Unconsciously incompetent

2. Consciously incompetent

3. Consciously competent

4. Unconsciously competent

Let's think back to being in a car as a young child in elementary school, looking out the window in the back seat, enjoying the ride, and listening to the music playing. We had no clue how to drive or what it would take to do so. This is the first stage of learning. In today's terms, we don't know what we don't know; it's called being unconsciously incompetent. We are not aware of how the car drives.

For most, the second stage begins as a young teen. It's the time when we become curious about how the car actually works and are aware that we don't know what it takes or how to drive. Now, we are fully aware that we don't know; we are consciously incompetent. It's interesting that at the end of this phase, we begin to pay attention to all the details because we want to learn.

This next phase begins when we get in the driver's seat with a learner's permit, or sooner for some, and we begin to practice all the rules we are taught, like buckling up, hand positioning, checking your rearview and side mirrors, looking over your shoulder when changing lanes, and a list of other to-dos. This is when we work on being consciously competent.

The last phase, which hopefully we are all at, is when you get in the car and do all the appropriate things without thinking about it. You know, driving with your knee on the steering wheel, eating a burger, listening to the radio blasting your favorite song, and all the while accomplishing all your to-dos. This is called being unconsciously competent. You can do it without thinking about it.

These stages of learning happen with every section you learn in this book. Some will be simple because you have been practicing them, and others will be downright nerve-racking because they are new to you. It's okay! We have all been there, and you will make it through each phase if you don't quit.

In a late-night conversation with a friend, the topic turned to personal development and growth. He expressed a common fear: "What if you're 50 and you think it's too late? What if you feel overwhelmed by everything you still need to work on or believe you've already learned all there is to know?" This question hits at the heart of the learning journey we've been discussing. It's crucial to confront and acknowledge where we truly stand in our path of growth, especially in relation to the four stages of learning we've explored.

The truth is, no matter our age, we're all navigating these stages in various aspects of our lives. In some areas, we might find ourselves unconsciously incompetent, blissfully unaware of what we don't know. In other cases, we may be painfully conscious of our incompetence, knowing there's much to learn. We may have reached the stage of conscious competence in certain skills, needing to remain focused and deliberate in our actions to maintain our proficiency. Ideally, we aspire to reach unconscious competence, where our skills become second nature without conscious thought.

Recognizing that this process never truly ends is key. Each stage offers its own lessons and opportunities for growth. Embracing where you are in the learning process without self-deception about your level of mastery, especially concerning the principles outlined in The 4D Method, is essential. This method, like the stages of learning, is a tool to guide us through the continuous journey of self-improvement.

Admitting to ourselves where we genuinely are in the learning process can be both a humbling and an empowering experience. It means acknowledging that, regardless of age or stage in life, we are all works in progress. There's always room for growth, for pushing through our fears, and for striving to reach our potential. By embracing the lessons of the four stages of learning, we can approach each new challenge with the understanding that it's okay to be at any stage in any area of our lives. The critical factor is our willingness to acknowledge it, learn from it, and move forward with the intention to grow. This mindset is what transforms the seemingly daunting journey of self-improvement into a rewarding path of continual learning and personal evolution.

REFLECTING ON YOUR CURRENT SKILLS
AND KNOWLEDGE, CAN YOU IDENTIFY
AN AREA OF YOUR LIFE WHERE YOU ARE
CURRENTLY IN THE PHASE OF BEING
"UNCONSCIOUSLY INCOMPETENT"? HOW
DOES RECOGNIZING THIS CHANGE YOUR
APPROACH TO LEARNING IN THAT AREA?

23

HOW RELATING TO OTHERS CAN BE PUT TO USE

"For as the body without the spirit is dead, so faith without works is dead also." James 2:26 (N.K.J.V.)

As we turn the page from gaining deep insights through situational intelligence and awareness, let's dive into how to apply what we have learned. Imagine taking those enlightening moments from others and yourself and making them work wonders in your relationships. From understanding to action, we now explore how insights become impactful through our deeds. Let's dive into how works, actions, and deeds transform our understanding into tangible change.

First, let's examine the words "works, action, and deeds" in the context of how relating to others can be useful.

In English translations of the Bible and other contexts, "works," "action," and "deeds" are terms often used interchangeably, each with its own unique meaning. Here's a clearer distinction between them:

Works: This term is often used to describe the outcomes or results of actions. For example, a completed piece of art or a project is considered a "work." It's tangible proof of effort and action. "Works" can also denote bodies of art or literature, subdividing them into creative, literary, and artistic works. These categories highlight the various outcomes that actions can produce.

Action: Contrary to "works," action refers to the act of doing something itself with a specific goal in mind. This involves the entire process, from planning and organizing to executing. Action is essentially the catalyst that initiates "works," akin to the spark that ignites a fire. The process of action emphasizes the importance of setting SMART goals to achieve specific results, acting as evidence of the work done. The effectiveness of actions is evaluated based on how well they meet these predefined goals.

Deeds: While "works" relate to the outcomes and "action" to the process, "deeds" specifically refer to actions taken or performed, often with a moral or ethical implication. Deeds are actions carried out with intention, typically reflecting the individual's character or intentions. In many contexts, deeds emphasize the ethical or moral weight of actions, highlighting their significance beyond mere activity.

For example, there's a popular advertisement in the home improvement world that labels their store as the place "where doers get things done." "Doing" represents the deed, the work, and the action, while "done" represents the accomplishment, the finished work. Faith, in this context, is the belief that our actions will culminate in a positive outcome.

Have you considered whether your image or your actions attract people like magnets or repel them? Your image identity is how others describe you, sometimes using physical features or characteristics such as "the tall guy with dark brown hair" or "she's the one that always dresses so professionally." At other times, you are described by your personality attributes or characteristics, for instance, "Oh, he's the nice guy in the second cubicle, always doing things for others, so friendly and kind," or perhaps, "You don't want to get close to him; he's mean and always in a bad mood." Image is significant.

Back in Jesus' day, a couple of individuals from the religious right attempted to ensnare Jesus with a question designed to undermine his popularity. They asked, in front of a crowd, whether taxes should be paid.

Jesus' response—asking for a Roman coin and inquiring whose image was on it—underscored a powerful principle: you belong to God and bear His image, reflecting His glory in your actions, words, and life's purpose. In today's world, where much revolves around image and identity, maintaining an image that reflects truth, integrity, honesty, and friendliness is crucial.

People form relationships with those they like, which is why learning about ourselves and being drawn to people similar to us is natural. **We are typically attracted to others for two main reasons: either their personality aligns with ours, or we admire qualities in them that we aspire to emulate.**

The golden rule, as spoken by Jesus, "Do unto others as you would have them do unto you," embodies a way of life that promotes kindness and compassion. Living by this principle naturally fosters positive relationships. Negative attitudes tend to isolate individuals, whereas positivity and optimism welcome camaraderie and companionship.

The Golden Rule can also apply to prospecting the people in our orbit using the Circle of Influence and Status.

Doing unto others as you would have them do unto you should be kept in the back of your mind as you begin to prospect for people you know or want to know and as you create interest, curiosity, help, or give direction between you and them.

There are three types of people in the below diagram about the circle of influence and status.

1. **The first type** consists of people we look up to. We should ask for their help, opinion, or a favor. This will usually yield the best results.

2. **The second type** consists of people who are equal to us in status and influence. Discuss the possibilities or opportunities of working together on a project. Also, remember to be normal and introduce them to an expert in the field. Make it about the opportunity, and never forget that people will travel miles to meet a person, but at times, they won't go across the street for an opportunity. Their first thought is that it's too good to be true. Communicate with them appropriately, depending on their personality or likes and dislikes.

3. **Lastly, the third type** consists of people who look up to us. For most of us, this is a smaller group of people, but this relationship has a strong influence, and you can usually tell this person what to do, and they will act.

Understanding these three differences can benefit you when talking with prospects. You can lead the conversation, be more relatable, and get them involved with some level of interest.

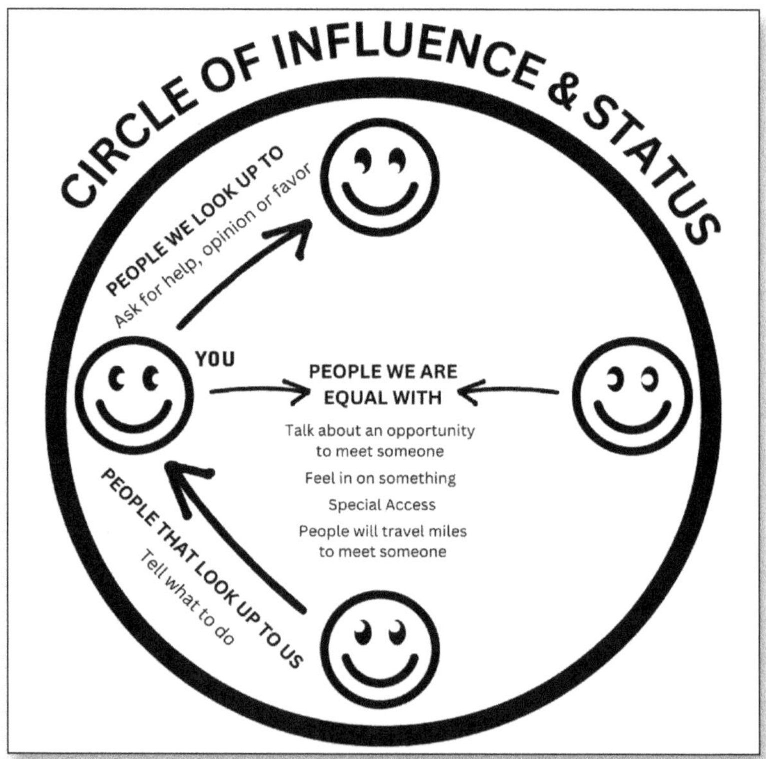

DIAGRAM SUBHEADING: The diagram is called the Circle of Influence and Status. Too often, we think of influence as being unidirectional: us influencing others. However, influence is multidirectional—up, down, right, and left. From every direction, there's an opportunity for influence, both from us and to us.

Careful here! When prospecting people, one common mistake is mis-categorizing them and not communicating with them at the appropriate level of the relationship. For example, talking to someone you admire as if they are on the same level as you would be a mistake. Another common mistake is assuming someone is your equal while they believe you should look up to them.

When building a bridge in a relationship, the other person's perception of reality matters most in developing trust and respect and in getting them to take action.

If you can't identify what type of person they are, it is best to treat them as the first type and look up to them. These are all ways of identifying people in our circle of influence and status.

Here is another example of how to build rapport when we meet new people. Let's use the acronym F.O.R.M. as a tool for asking discovery questions.

F.O.R.M. (Family. Occupation. Recreation. Motivation)

This method is a straightforward way to make conversations more interesting and connect on a deeper level. Here's a practical guide to using it:

- **Family:** Start by asking, "Do you have siblings or a large family? What are they like?" It's a great way to start conversations and learn about their background and family dynamics.

- **Occupation:** Move on to "What led you to your current job?" This question opens up discussions about career paths, passions, and some mutual professional interests or experiences.

- **Recreation:** Ask, "What do you like to do for fun?" This allows you to discover shared interests or hobbies, which can lead to more engaging discussions about how they spend their free time.

- **Motivation:** Finish with, "What's something you've always wanted to achieve, and why?" This encourages them to share their aspirations and motivations, allowing for a deeper understanding and connection.

When using F.O.R.M., the goal is to encourage open dialogue, show genuine interest in the other person's responses, and look for common ground to enrich the conversation—genuinely helping them get more of what they want and less of what they don't.

The unlimited currency in life is the relationships you have access to, which can be utilized for a variety of reasons, including social, community, spiritual, or business endeavors. Be as serious about developing a list of people you have built or want to build relationships with as a heart surgeon learning how to perform surgery. It could be a life-or-death situation in the future.

There is a process and a way things need to be done to have a positive outcome. This process is delicate at times and requires your complete attention. The more you try to wing it, the less likely you are to succeed. One relationship can literally change your life.

I heard a long time ago, "Some will, some won't, so what? Next!" I understand the sentiment of having thick skin and the mentality of keeping moving forward, looking for someone who will follow you in any endeavor.

But, it is shortsighted to throw spaghetti against the wall to see what sticks. It is far more valuable to form relationships with people and help each other get to where you want to go in life. I am not only recommending this process; I live it. Of course, I have made mistakes here and there, and I continually sharpen my skills to get better, and so should you!

In my early 20s, when I was first made aware of this technique, it was rare to get 100 people on a relationship list. Today, I have thousands on my list. It is amazing what you can accomplish when you build the right relationships with the right intentions. Here is an example of how to develop a relationship list and how to put it to use:

Rank	Name	Ph#/Email	Co.	Title	City/St.	Affiliation?
1						
2						
3						

The real value in creating a list is not just in the names; it's in how you cultivate these relationships. Your intention should always be to make your interactions mutually beneficial.

Rank on a Scale of 1-5:

1. **Very close relationship:** If you knocked on their door, they would invite you in, and both of you would feel totally comfortable—especially if you've slept over at their house or fallen asleep there.

2. **Still a strong relationship:** This is more business and less personal. They may stop by your home to pick you up, but all of the meetings are in public. They are definitely not sleeping over.

3. **Strictly public acquaintance:** You have good relationships, but they are based on motives and reasons.

4. **Acquaintance:** You know each other but may never have been formally introduced.

5. **Cold contact:** This person is unknown to you when it comes to building a relationship.

The next steps in building your network include gathering the following details about each contact:

Name: How they are formally addressed.

Phone/Email: Essential contact methods.

Company: Where they are employed.

Title: Their role within the company.

City/State: Geographic location is helpful for understanding their local context.

Affiliation: How you know them helps frame your relationship.

This information is crucial for developing relationships. It provides insight into how to communicate effectively by integrating several key concepts:

Circle of Influence & Status

Personality Profiles

Understanding Society

Building Rapport through our F.O.R.M. acronym

Each attribute you gather will aid you, through time and practice, in becoming an outstanding communicator.

Historically, some of the most successful individuals in the world, such as the Rockefeller, Kennedy, and Vanderbilt families, meticulously collected this kind of information using a Rolodex. While the Rolodex may now be obsolete, replaced by smartphones and spreadsheets, the essence of this process remains invaluable for anyone looking to foster meaningful connections.

HAVE YOU EVER HAD AN "AHA" MOMENT
ABOUT SOMEONE THAT CHANGED
HOW YOU INTERACT WITH THEM? HOW
CAN YOU USE SIMILAR REVELATIONS
TO STRENGTHEN YOUR CURRENT
RELATIONSHIPS?

24

HOW ENDORSABLE AM I?

"What is your reputation with yourself and others?"
—David Lloyd Strauss

Drawing inspiration from Daniel's story in the Old Testament, we're confronted with a timeless inquiry: "Are you endorsable?" Are you known for your positive character and integrity? Daniel's experiences, from his dietary defiance to his unwavering faith among lions, serve as a mirror for our own life choices and the integrity of our convictions. As we explore Daniel's journey, we are prompted to scrutinize the principles we hold dear and the compromises we refuse to make. Are our actions today such that we would earn endorsement not only from others but also from ourselves?

Stepping aside from the history of Daniel and moving to the New Testament, we find a resounding message in 2 Timothy 3:1-2 ESV, highlighting the enduring challenge of living with virtue in trying times. This passage serves as a stark reminder:

"But understand this: In the last days, there will come times of difficulty. People will be lovers of themselves, lovers of money, proud, arrogant, abusive, disobedient to their parents, ungrateful, unholy."

These words encourage us to evaluate our own lives in the context of today's world, urging us to be the kind of individuals who are, indeed, endorsable.

Every generation has witnessed behavior as described in the above scripture. Every generation voices its disappointment in the next, longing for the way things used to be. My father used to say, "They sure don't make people these days like they used to." Since the beginning of time, Earth has always had good people and bad people, smart people and not-so-smart people, and right people and wrong people. Rather than complaining about the negatives in people, it's always better to shine your light.

Imagine living in Daniel's day. Your people, the chosen people of God, have just been taken into captivity. It's hard to imagine China taking control of the United States, but that would be equivalent to Israel being taken captive by the Babylonian empire.

Babylon was home to the famous "hanging gardens," one of the seven wonders of the ancient world. King Nebuchadnezzar transformed Babylon into one of the most splendid cities of the ancient world. Nebuchadnezzar conquered Assyria, Egypt, and Judah, but his most famous conquest was Jerusalem.

He was a ruthless, cruel king known for piling the dead bodies of his victims outside of his city walls as a display and declaration of his mighty victories. He not only destroyed Jerusalem but also forced the Jewish people into exile. Nebuchadnezzar's destruction of cities was so fierce, and the fires so hot that they turned limestone buildings into lime. His military conquests made him one of history's greatest kings; you didn't question his leadership, and you obeyed his every command.

Bible scholars suggest that Daniel was between the ages of 13 and 16. He was in a new land, hand-selected to serve this cruel heathen King, given a new name, new clothes, new rules, and no chance for escape; obedience was his only means of survival.

Daniel's dilemma: the food he's ordered to eat is not kosher. Daniel is in a covenantal relationship with God. If he chooses to eat the King's food, he defiles himself in God's eyes. If he doesn't eat the King's food, he dies. So, what would you do?

If you think this is no big deal or that God should cut him some slack, that's probably where some of our problems come from. Our convictions become preferences when they're no longer convenient to keep. You choose your convictions, and they are very different from your preferences. We may prefer to live a more moral or noble life, but if it's inconvenient, we tend to compromise.

Daniel's decision not to eat the King's delicacies was non-negotiable. Everyone should have some non-negotiables. These are internal convictions that are not swayed or adjusted by outside conditions; they are deep-seated choices made with a sense of obligation and promises made to ourselves with the commitment to keep them.

What Daniel decides to do would be unheard of, so he asks for a kosher meal. He gets what he asks for, and because of his choice, God gifted him with favor, knowledge, insight, and understanding beyond anyone serving the King. The lesson for us is to determine today what is non-negotiable and stick to it. Before you're tempted or tested, make a wise choice with your internal compass and stay on course.

If you're wondering if this is the same Daniel, the answer is yes. This is the same Daniel who wouldn't bow down to the King's idol and the same Daniel who was thrown into the lion's den. Each time, he was rescued and redeemed by God, with blessings that followed because he chose to live a life without compromise.

Around 800 BC, Isaiah the prophet declared in Isaiah 5:20 NIV:

"Woe to them that call evil good and good evil, that put darkness for light and light for darkness, and that put bitter for sweet and sweet for bitter."

It's amazing to me how applicable that proclamation is today. Yes, we are living in a very upside-down world; sin is no longer sin—it is "freedom." Truth is no longer truth—it's "opinion." There is no right or wrong; it's simply a matter of how you feel.

As I read the word "Woe" by the prophet, I thought about its dictionary definition, "great sorrow or distress," but I also thought of the "whoa" when we ride a horse—meaning to slow or stop.

When I consider these together, I ask myself: Am I the type of person perpetuating global sorrow and distress, or am I on a horse of truth for Jesus saying, "WHOA?" Slow down. Stop. Let's think before we act.

It would be great if we could reverse the course of so much of the cruel and criminal behavior happening today and somehow arrest the attitudes that are so prevalent: anti-God, anti-truth, and anti-righteousness. To be an endorsable person in the eyes of God would be the best choice, wouldn't it?

If we were to take a play out of Daniel's book, we could choose to act like him and live the kind of life that he did. Now think HONORABLE man, VIRTUOUS woman. Not just another person but a person with internal values that are externally expressed. A lack of those characteristics can be costly.

Tiger Woods is a more recent example of how important honor and virtue are. I have always been impressed with Tiger Woods' skill and talent; he is truly one of the very best at the game of golf. However, years ago, in a battle with personal choices, he found himself embarrassed and humiliated by an arrest, which was the result of his questionable behavior.

It's been estimated that his revenue loss from his major sponsors dropping him cost him between 30 and 40 million dollars. OUCH!

There is a good chance that would not have happened if he had confided in accountable friendships and partnerships with the kind of people who were free to speak into his life—true friends who were looking out for his best interests. I promise you; it would have been a game-changer.

So now look at your life: Are you endorsable? When you go back to Daniel's big events, you will notice he had friends by his side: Shadrach, Meshach, and Abednego. On each occasion, he made a pact, each holding the other accountable for keeping their commitments to remain faithful. Daniel is endorsable, so much so that after the "lion's den" event, when he was placed in a den full of lions and came out unscathed in the morning, King Nebuchadnezzar decreed that everyone should follow Daniel's God because He's the real God!

It's awe-inspiring how Daniel kept his commitment to God, which impacted and influenced one of history's more wicked leaders. Consider living the kind of life that is so admired and respected that it is your God that others choose to follow when they see the light that you live in and the freedom you enjoy.

Think about Daniel's character from another perspective. If you're hoping to find that special someone and they meet your last girlfriend or boyfriend, was your past behavior honorable, truthful, and respectful?

If you're hoping to get that promotion, would your current team be puzzled to see you move upward? If questioned, would they say it surprised them because you were such a bad example of what a good employee should be?

An endorsable person lives their life based on principles. Daniel's convictions didn't change with the wind or shift with the current. It can be done.

The Bible records for us these words: "...and Daniel chose in his heart not to defile himself." It was a choice. Today, you can make yours.

REFLECTING ON DANIEL'S STORY OF INTEGRITY AND STEADFAST FAITH, HOW DO YOU ENSURE YOUR DAILY ACTIONS ALIGN WITH THE VIRTUES YOU BELIEVE IN, SO THAT OTHERS MIGHT SEE THEM AS AUTHENTIC AND ENDORSE YOUR CHARACTER?

WHY DO RELATIONSHIPS HAVE ULTIMATE VALUE?

When most people think about relationships, they refer to their relationships with others, but there are really three key categories of relationships: with ourselves, others, and God.

The Christian cross serves as a profound analogy for understanding the interconnectedness of our relationships. The horizontal beam symbolizes our relationships with others—our peers, family, friends, and the broader community. It represents our day-to-day interactions and the earthly, outward connections we forge.

The vertical beam points upward, symbolizing our relationship with Jesus. This line is a direct and personal channel between the individual and God, highlighting the spiritual and transcendent nature of this relationship.

At the intersection of these two beams lies the heart of the analogy—the point where we stand. This junction represents us as individuals, uniquely positioned at the crossroads of our earthly relationships and our spiritual connection with God. It underscores the idea that our spiritual life deeply influences our interactions with others and that our relationships with others can reflect our relationship with God. This intersection invites a harmonious approach to life, emphasizing the importance of nurturing both dimensions to fully realize our spiritual inheritance and live meaningfully with others.

Our Relationship With Ourselves

How's your relationship with yourself? Do you believe in yourself? Are your thoughts about yourself positive or negative?

Your relationship with yourself is paramount. Through this book, you have started to understand why you are who you are. You can choose to make adjustments anytime! Don't put it off any longer. God has blessed you with gifts, talents, abilities, and skills that must be developed by your own choice and effort.

2 Timothy 1:6-7 says:

"This is why I remind you to fan into flames the spiritual gift God gave you when I laid my hands on you. For God has not given us a spirit of fear and timidity but of power, love, and self-discipline."

Sharpening our gifts, talents, abilities, and skills to serve the people around us honors God.

Many people waste those gifts because they are indecisive or wishy-washy. Think about it: how many times do we say we are going to do something and don't do it or stop halfway through? We may have good intentions, but ultimately, we are lying to ourselves because we don't have the mental strength to follow through. And so, we develop a habit of self-deceit. It is amazing how easily we become conditioned to stop believing in the commitments we make to ourselves.

This type of self-sabotage is frightening, and it usually stems from a fear of something we haven't addressed.

Let's say we got over that fear today and started doing what we say we are going to do—one commitment at a time. Each commitment builds on the next and gives us more confidence in our commitment to ourselves.

For example, what is it going to take for you to really commit to taking care of your body, mind, and spirit? Are you treating life like a big present, eager to open every day? If not, why not? It's your choice to take control of your thoughts and commitments.

From now on, when you feel the slightest hesitation about not following through with what you committed to, take a deep breath, say a quick prayer, and ask God to help you respond with resolve to stay the course. That perseverance until completion will fill you with joy, optimism, and hope! That is a prescription for a life with unlimited possibilities.

Our Relationship With the People Around Us

Let's talk about the people around us. Ask yourself if you are good to the people God has put in your path. Are you too self-centered? How kind, compassionate, respectful, and caring are you? Have you considered their feelings and expectations? I've learned through many mistakes that unmet expectations always lead to resentment because of a lack of clear communication. How can you expect those qualities from others if you don't display them?

Remember earlier in the book when we discussed the second greatest commandment of God, which is loving our neighbor as ourselves? We must take this to heart and consider how we treat the people around us. We also thoroughly discussed how to understand the personalities of people around us, the categories of society people fit into, and how to communicate with people better because we take time to understand their point of view! All of these things can help you love your neighbor.

At times, loving our neighbors is challenging, especially when they are very different from us. Doing so requires guidance from Jesus' behavior. The Word of God gives great insight into this:

"Love is patient and kind. Love is not jealous, boastful, proud, or rude. It does not demand its own way. It is not irritable, and it keeps no record of being wronged. It does not rejoice over injustice, but it rejoices when the truth prevails. Love never gives up, never loses faith, is always hopeful, and endures through every circumstance."
—*1 Corinthians 13:4-7 (NLT)*

Do the people around you cheer you on or knock you down? People who really want to see you win in some way are willing to help you win! If your life is affected by who you spend time with, shouldn't you be careful about who you hang around? Your close relationships should be mutually beneficial, and each person should be eager to help the other. If not, then they are one-sided, and someone is taking advantage of you. I wouldn't like that, and neither should you.

I'm not saying every person you come in contact with needs to give you something in return; a kind gesture with no expectations is fine, and helping someone in need is the right thing to do. I am saying, don't get taken advantage of by people who are capable and are just using you.

Lou Holtz said: "There is never a right time to do the wrong thing, and there is never a wrong time to do the right thing!"

LOU HOLTZ · ANNELIESE · DERRICK

If you need to make new friends or be a better friend, do it! Life is too short to waste time not putting your best foot forward.

Our Relationship With God

Remember The 4D Method from Chapter 12? I'm sure you recall how it resembled a target for ease of understanding and clarity, providing areas of development we can aim toward.

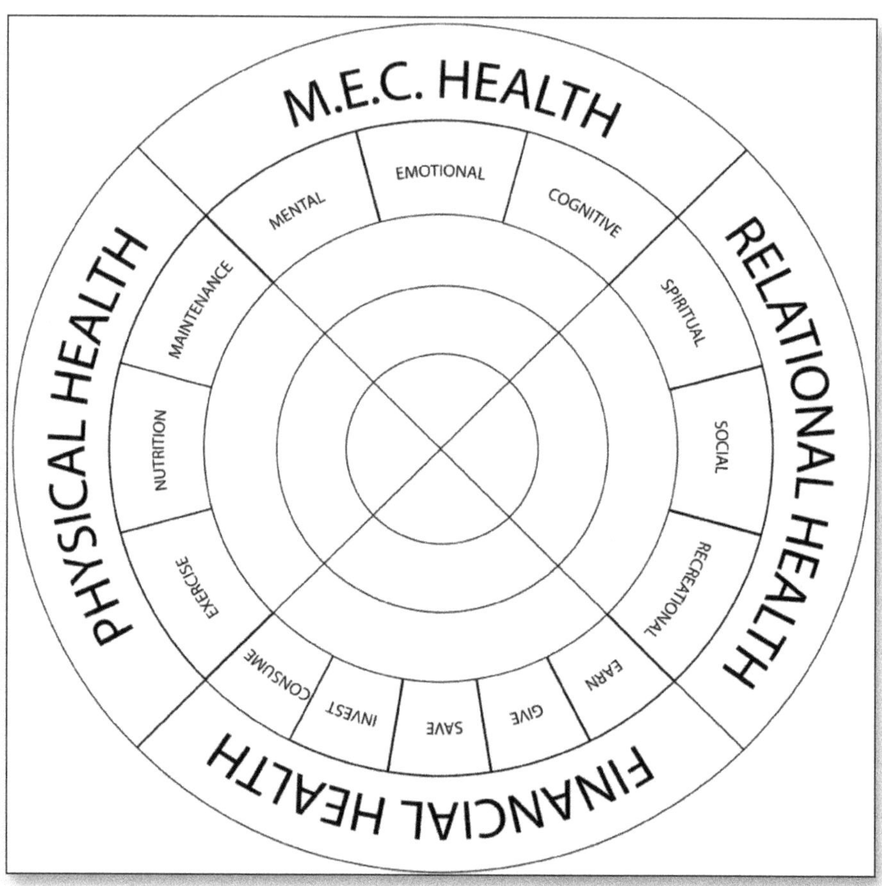

Now, as a well-informed reader, the next step is to view The 4D Method as a raw clay plate that represents each one of us as we enter this world with the ability to carry out all the developmental areas of our lives.

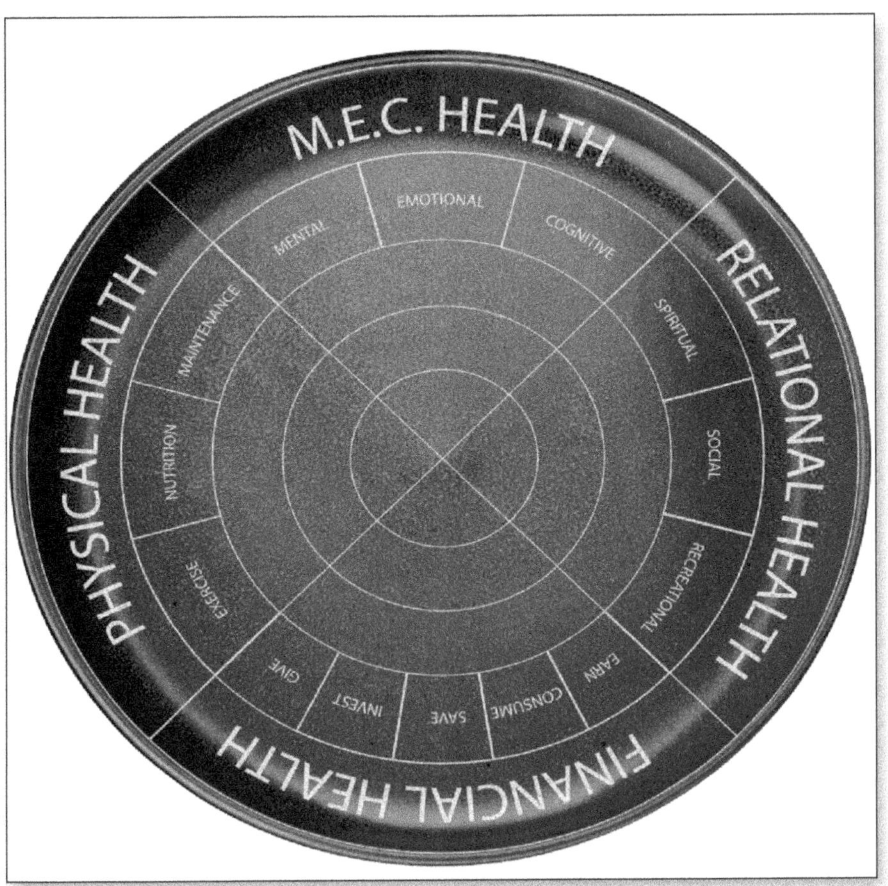

Over time, we do our best to perfect that plate. Most of us aim to make it stronger in all areas and, let's not forget, more beautiful. Depending on how we strengthen or neglect each of those areas, it can cause the plate to become stronger or weaker and potentially break into pieces. Paying attention to this requires a delicate balance of awareness and effort.

Have you ever felt like that broken plate? Have you ever said to yourself that something doesn't feel right and needs to be fixed but can't quite identify it? When this happens, we naturally look for a solution to fix it or ignore it, letting things worsen if we ignore it. Trust me, it's better to fix it. How do we do that? We can do this by first praying and acknowledging that we need God's help, then giving Him the broken pieces of the plate. God, the ultimate creator or potter, will help you fix the weak spots and put your life back together better than when you gave those broken pieces to Him.

Once you do that, you start to see dramatic changes in yourself, and the world will take notice of your transformation—the version of yourself that only the potter could have displayed through you.

The color logo on the front of the book, with gold running through the cracks, represents God providing a way to put us back together. It is an intertwined relationship between us and God to repair the cracks. This unique relationship produces the transformation that changes us. It changes how the plate looks, the strength of what it can handle, and its ability to be used to serve the people it comes into contact with. This process transforms the plate from broken pieces to a MASTERPIECE only God could repair.

Jesus is the ultimate MASTERPIECE—He's our Savior because that's what He does; He saves us. What does he save us from? OUR-SELVES. God harnesses and arrests our selfish desires and sinful attitudes. What a relationship this is!

CONSIDERING YOUR SPIRITUAL
RELATIONSHIP, HOW OFTEN DO YOU
EVALUATE WHETHER YOUR ACTIONS
ALIGN WITH YOUR SPIRITUAL BELIEFS,
AND HOW DO THESE BELIEFS INFLUENCE
YOUR RELATIONSHIPS WITH OTHERS AND
YOURSELF?

BONUS CHAPTER

A close friend related a story to me about an encounter he had years ago with the head of a hospice center. She had started in hospice care as a nurse and worked her way up to a senior position. Curiously, he asked her, "How did you get into hospice care?" She replied that while she was still serving as a nurse, she cared for a patient who died alone. Then she said something he'd never forget: "No one should die alone." On his nightstand was a Rolex watch, and under the stand was a very expensive pair of designer shoes. One must wonder if his business life made him successful, but his priorities kept him from doing the things that should have mattered more—people. Why does that happen?

As I reflected on the story, I wondered, where are the friends—the business associates, the golf buddies, the fishing friends? Certainly, I won't assume that our lack of friendliness created an environment of aloneness, but I contrast that with being with a man just a few weeks ago who was in his final days. A group of us surrounded him at his bedside, singing worship songs and praying for him as he faded from this life to the next.

As we age, it's common to fear being alone. We live in a very transient society, where our friends and loved ones move and change jobs, get divorced, and start over, and many times, our relationships are lost in the shuffle.

At the beginning of this book, you might have thought, "Another self-help book." I hope what you have come to realize is that having a better awareness of ourselves allows us to give more grace and understanding to our neighbors. Loving our neighbor and using our gifts, talents, and abilities to serve each other is part of what Jesus meant when He said, "Love your neighbor as yourself."

Jesus makes it clear that we should first love God with all our heart, soul, and mind and then love our neighbor as ourselves. I AM created you as a one-of-a-kind MASTERPIECE. This book is a practical guide to help you build a better relationship with your neighbors (work or personal). Realize that it's never too late for a second chance, and no matter how many times we fall, our Father in Heaven hurts when we fall and cheers when we overcome a challenge or are triumphant with a goal! Don't ever forget that you were made in His image.

Every one of us is looking to experience hope, love, joy, and peace. Just a ray of hope can fill us with optimism on this journey of life and instill an internal feeling of saying, "I can do it!" In addition to that, hope is always coupled with wonder. You are instilled with a supernatural wonder about the possibility that your circumstances can change for the better. As people of faith, the expectation of something more is a motivator filled with trust. God is good all the time.

True love fills our hearts and is unconditional when based on what the scriptures say about the way God loves us. The Greek word AGAPE has been used a number of times, and it refers to the supreme or superior kind of love that is not predicated on what we do for God but rather on what He has done for us.

Joy is an emotion that is not necessarily based on our environment or the circumstances in which we may find ourselves. Joy is very different from happiness, which follows a reason to be happy; joy is more of an internal awareness of well-being. When we know that God has us in His hand, His plans are linked to His faithfulness, which has been experienced and embraced from person to person, from generation to generation.

The Bible says this in Romans 8:28: "And we know that in ALL things God works for the GOOD of those who love Him, who have been called according to His purpose."

Finally, peace is the thing that isn't typically talked about or explained in a way that reveals what we believe to be the essence of what we long for and desire. The reason for writing this book has more to do with you finding your personal peace than anything else. When you find your where you fit in in this world and are performing in that "sweet spot," you're naturally going to put your head on the pillow at night with a sigh of relief, knowing that where you are is exactly where you are supposed to be.

When you have given it your best, yielding to your Master's hand, and you are allowing Him to mold, shape, transform, and change you, even directing your life to the best place for you. When you know you're in the right relationships, you're working at a place where you feel valued and appreciated when the place you live is more than a house but a home, and when you are able to say in your heart, "It is well with my soul," you have found it! No longer comparing your life to someone else's, filled with jealousy or envy, you get to a place where you know you wouldn't trade your life for anyone else's because it's yours, and your best friend, God, is leading the way, and you're filled with genuine excitement, looking forward to what He has in mind.

Now, before you close the book, there is one more imperative truth that must be shared. The devil exists, and he has a plan for you too! Evidence of that fact is expressed every day, everywhere around the globe. Jesus warned His followers of the enemy's mission: He (the devil) has come to kill, steal, and destroy. Whenever you attempt to do anything worthwhile, noble, or righteous, you'll find him lurking in the shadows, like a poisonous spider in its web, with the silk spread in every direction, just being patient, trusting that at some point you'll make contact. The enemy is cunning and subtle, trying to convince you using doubt and fear with the hope you will drift away from your relationship with God and His Word. When this happens, you find yourself off-track and wondering how you got to this place.

Please know that the Word of God is powerful and unifies a relationship between you and your Maker, who is weaving together a plan greater than you can even imagine. He will never leave you or forsake you. In Revelation 3:20, Jesus said, "Here I am! I stand at the door and knock. If anyone hears my voice and opens the door, I will come in..." He wants access; it's an inside job. It's the best decision you will ever make, but you are the only one who can give Him a way in. It requires repentance—a simple confession of your desire to live life according to His plan.

If you don't have a personal relationship with Jesus yet, or maybe it is time for a recommitment:

Are you ready to turn to Jesus to be your Savior, your friend, and your One True God? Romans 10:9 says, "If you confess with your mouth that Jesus is Lord and believe in your heart that God raised him from the dead, you will be saved."

Use your own words to express your feelings sincerely. You can't pull a scam on God; He knows your heart. Ask Him something like this:

Dear God, I want to receive you in my life as my God, Savior, and Friend. I understand Jesus came to earth, died on the cross, and rose from the dead, all on my behalf to completely take care of my problem of sin and give me eternal life.

Please, forgive me of my sins and help me to follow You all the days of my life, from this day forever. Amen.

Psalm 103:12 "As far as the east is from the west, so far has He removed our sins from us."

Joshua 1:9 "Have I not commanded you? Be strong and courageous. Do not be afraid; Do not be discouraged, for the Lord your God will be with you wherever you go."

QUESTIONS?

If you have any questions, please email us at questions@ iam2ndchances.org

PRAYER REQUESTS?

If you have any prayer requests, email us at: prayer@ iam2ndchances.org

CURIOUS ABOUT JESUS?

For more information on your relationship with God through his son Jesus, please go to: www.iam2ndchances.org

JOIN THE BIBLE STUDY

Now that you have completed your personal journey through "I AM MASTERPIECE," I invite you to continue exploring the transformative insights and teachings within a Bible study or small group setting. This book isn't just a personal guide; it's a tool for communal growth and spiritual enrichment.

By integrating the principles from "I AM MASTERPIECE" into your group discussions and teachings, you can deepen your collective understanding and strengthen your walk with God together. Let each chapter serve as a springboard for deeper reflection, discussion, and application within your communities. Discover together how each of us is uniquely a MASTERPIECE, living out God's divine artistry.

INTERESTED IN THE BIBLE STUDY?

If interested in our bible study, please email us at:

biblestudy@IAMMasterpiece.com

COMMUNITY INVITATION

Join the Voyage of Self-Discovery

Through these pages, we've embarked on a voyage of self-discovery, acknowledging that we are indeed a MASTERPIECE in the eyes of God, sculpted with divine intention and purpose. Each chapter has been a brushstroke on the canvas of our existence, revealing how our complexities and simplicities come together to form a picture that is both a work in progress and a complete work of art in the hands of God.

We've uncovered the layers of our identity, the nurture and nature of our being, and the gates through which we interact with the world. We've considered the influences that shape us, the intrinsic drive to learn, and the undeniable role that Jesus plays in our development. Our personal and professional growth, the significance of our relationships, the stewardship of our time, the wisdom in seeking guidance, and the courage to lead—all these themes come together in a life that seeks to honor Jesus' teachings.

The fabric of this book—woven with threads of mental, emotional, cognitive, and physical health, financial wisdom, and relational depth—demonstrates that our value is not just in the sum of our parts but in the intentionality with which we live. The SMART goals, personality insights, societal understanding, and every stage of learning are tools given to us to hone our God-given potential.

As we apply what we've learned, we recognize our "endorse ability—our ability to be authentic ambassadors of Christ's love through our actions and relationships. We're invited to see ourselves as God sees us, embrace our inherent worth, and act accordingly, doing the good works He has planned for us.

So, as we conclude, let's not merely close the cover of a book but open the next chapter of our lives with renewed vision. We are called to be Jesus' hands and feet, reflecting His grace in our growth. Our MASTERPIECE status isn't a static accolade but a living, breathing testament to the ongoing creative process that is our life in Christ. Embrace it, nurture it, and step forward in the confidence that God is with you, perfecting His MASTERPIECE every day.

Here are three hands-on challenges that invite you to live out your identity as a MASTERPIECE created by God. This is your invitation to action—practical steps to weave the grand tapestry of teachings into the fabric of your daily life. Embrace these tasks as personal milestones on your journey to growth, knowing that with each step, you embody the work and wonder of divine artistry. Are you ready to step into this? Your journey starts now.

If you are eager to sculpt a life that reflects your true potential, join the "I AM MASTERPIECE COMMUNITY" and start your transformation with these thought-provoking questions:

- **Discovery**: Which chapters resonated deeply with you and sparked a desire for change?

- **Action**: Inspired by the insights, what specific changes are you ready to implement in your life?

- **Guidance**: If you could choose one area of your life mentioned in this book to enhance with expert guidance, which would it be?

The community is not just about finding answers—it's about discovering your path to unveil the MASTERPIECE you are made to be.

Join the I AM MASTERPIECE Community

IAMMASTERPIECE.COM

AFTERWORD
FROM MY BEAUTIFUL BRIDE, ANNELIESE

While I was sitting in a hospital room, staring at the picture of the human heart anatomy with all my husband's blockages mapped out like hidden treasures, I was in sheer disbelief at how many there were. Looking back on that day almost a year and a half ago, I realize how good God truly is in all things, remembering the peace He gave me and knowing it wasn't the end of Derrick's story. God still had so much in store for him to complete. Overcoming a heart attack and quadruple bypass surgery was just one of many challenges Derrick has faced in his life, or perhaps I should say—great triumphs he has achieved.

Having written this book is surprising, but also, "Of course you wrote a book." After all, God put it on your heart to do this. He gave you these thoughts, and I watched as He led you down a path, guiding every step you took to complete it. You didn't write this book during a period of calm; you wrote it during a very challenging and transformative time in our lives. You started while still recovering from that quadruple bypass, regaining your strength and basic life abilities, all while helping our son graduate from high school and move overseas to Madrid, Spain, for college and soccer. We also sold everything, packed up, and moved from Indiana to Florida, then moved a second time within Florida in just three- and one-half months. Those are just some of the highlights of the challenges we overcame together while you were writing this book.

God is good. Here we are, with this literal masterpiece—born of blood, sweat, tears, and a lifetime of learning, overcoming, and triumphing—finally complete. I am in awe and so proud of you. Am I shocked? Not really. When Derrick says he is going to do something, when he puts his mind to it, especially when God has put it in his heart, it will be completed.

ANNELIESE

ANNELISE AND DERRICK

ANNELIESE · DANNY · DERRICK

ACKNOWLEDGMENTS

As I reflect on the journey that brought this book to fruition, my heart is filled with immense gratitude for the incredible circle of support that surrounded me. The creation of this book was a deeply personal and spiritual endeavor, guided by the hand of God and enriched by the contributions of many who stood by me over the course of a year. I want to extend my heartfelt thanks to each person who played a pivotal role in shaping this work into what God intended it to be. Your encouragement, insights, and faith in this project have been nothing short of a blessing.

David Lloyd Strauss — You are such a great coach and teacher. I loved your editing style for three main reasons: your vocabulary is exemplary, yet you use analogies to get your points across; you're assertive and get things done but remain kind; and lastly, you exude compassion and strength! Keep being you, David. You are the best investment an author could make for help through every phase of book development and publishing advice.

Michael Franzese — God sure had an awesome plan for our lives, but if it were left up to us, we would have messed it up, wouldn't we? I'm so thankful we had a providential meeting 12 years ago— God knows what He is doing! You have always stuck by my side, no matter how many ups and downs I went through. Keep being you, Michael. You're a great friend, mentor, and brother in Christ!

Anneliese Serianni — You are sunshine inside and out. Your unwavering love for Jesus makes me strive to be a better husband, father, and friend. I'm so thankful you are my partner.

Gary Rees — Some would call us friends; I would say that's an understatement. Being "back-to-back" is more like it! Thank you for being someone I have always been able to count on—you are one of the most generous humans I know.

R.J.C. — Thank you for helping me express and expand all my thoughts in a way that would encapsulate what I wanted to explain to my son and now to the world.

I will never forget these simple statements that have been extremely motivating to me: 1 Corinthians 2:9 (NKJV): "No eye has seen, nor ear heard, nor has it entered into the heart of man, the things which God has prepared for those who love Him."

This year, your heart has never been more prepared and changed, and God is now prepared to use that heart to change the hearts of countless thousands! We are honored and blessed to have been and continue to be connected to your amazing heart!! Your B.F.F.

Beth Serafin — You are an amazing prayer partner, consistent in your love for Jesus, and passionate about providing care for families that suffer from DIPG. Beth, you played a pivotal role in helping me bring this book to life, and I won't forget it.

Kirk Allaire — Thank you so much for always checking in on me and my family. You have been a great source of encouragement and an amazing sounding board with which to think things out. God definitely had a plan when He providentially had our paths crossed over 12 years ago.

Richard Eskra — Your support, training, and friendship were so helpful to me! I will never forget how you supported me and my family before, during, and after recovery. I am always here for you, no matter what.

Roger Goranson — Thanks for being a true friend and confidant. No matter how "rough around the edges" you may portray yourself, I have always seen that Jesus is on your mind and that you are concerned about knowing Him better.

Teresa Mattone — You have become like family to us; in mob terms, you are definitely our consigliere! Your advice has always been clear, thoughtful, and aimed at achieving the best outcome. Your love and supportive attitude ooze out of all that you are. My wife and I are so thankful you are in our lives.

Nick Palumbo — Your guidance and encouragement have been instrumental in this project. You're a wonderful person who is always in pursuit of knowing and displaying Jesus in all you do.

Landon Meadows — Thank you for your friendship and coaching in this endeavor. Your love for Jesus is evident—keep it up!

Jay Emma — Thank you for your encouragement, laughter, and always being willing to lend a helping hand!

Nolan & Tiffany Passick — After over 25 years of friendship, I am so thankful for both of your love and support. Anne and I will never forget your trips to the hospital and bringing meals to our house while I was in recovery.

Ralph & Joi Rodriguez — My wife and I couldn't imagine living without you guys. Thanks so much for your unconditional love and support. You both always made us feel at home. We love you and your whole family!

Ralph & Janis Bornemann — You both have always been supportive, loving, and optimistic. I am so grateful for your love for Jesus. Oh, by the way, my wife is pretty awesome too!

Russ & Anna Bettis — Your friendship is something we cherish deeply. A lot of this book was created from your place in Florida, and we are so thankful you gave us a place to call home.

Lisa Schmidt — One of the hardest workers I know and always willing to make a great deal! I'm excited to see where this book takes us. Thank you for everything—you're the coolest and most reliable agent I know!

Mark Eric — I am so grateful for your expertise in audiobooks. I listen to them often, and now you're making my book come to life.

Corey Carbon — Thank you for taking the time to review the entire book and audiobook with me for weeks. You are a true friend and confidant. I appreciate all your support!

Clint Carney — There has always been an unspeakable bond and unconditional love between us. Whether we agree or not, on any subject, doesn't matter. Thank you for showing the world around us the amazing amount of sacrifice you displayed raising your son. It inspired me more than you know.

TO MY MOM & SIBLINGS

Anita Serianni (my mom) — Your love and support throughout my life allowed me to learn and grow in a way that was imperative to writing this book. Thank you for all your sacrifices, including raising me the best you knew how.

Anita "Nini" Rinaldis — I learned a lot from you from afar. Your class and desire to want more and better out of life are qualities I love about you.

Dan "Boo-Boo" Serianni — You are someone I've always had a deep love for. Your relentless work ethic is to be admired. I will never forget that you made it to the hospital in Indiana before the open-heart surgery from N.Y.

Catherine "Kay-Kay" Young — I think between you and Grandma Deal, I learned my love for music and singing. Your passion for music and lyrics was undeniable.

Louisa "Lou-Lou" Piguet — You are one of the hardest-working people I know, and you are loving and kind beyond words.

Maureen "Moe" Serianni — As my closest sibling in age, you have always had my back. I'm so thankful for your love, support, competitiveness, and your unwavering love for Danny Boy. You have always been there for me.

ABOUT DERRICK SERIANNI

Derrick Serianni is an inspirational author, speaker, and guide who has embraced his second chance at life with profound passion and dedication. After surviving a heart attack and undergoing quadruple bypass surgery, Derrick deepened his walk with Jesus, allowing this spiritual renewal to transform every aspect of his life.

His writings and speeches are rooted in this journey of recovery and faith, focusing on self-awareness, resilience, and the power of relationships. Derrick's approach is personable and motivational, connecting deeply with readers and audiences by sharing insights and practical advice from his own life experiences.

Derrick fervently believes in the power of second chances and the importance of living a life that faithfully reflects one's values and spiritual beliefs. He combines practical life lessons with biblical principles, encouraging his readers to lead lives that are successful, spiritually enriched, and aligned with their faith.

In his books and presentations, Derrick advocates for a life infused with personal well-being and spiritual growth, emphasizing the significance of nurturing relationships and building a supportive community that uplifts and sustains. His commitment to his faith is evident as he encourages others to cultivate a closer relationship with Jesus, seeing this as the foundation for a transformative and fulfilling life.

Whether through written words or engaging talks, Derrick Serianni offers guidance and inspiration for navigating life's complexities with courage, faith, and a heart open to God's direction. He inspires his audience to seize their day-to-day experiences as opportunities for spiritual and personal growth, drawing on their inner strength and the power of their faith to live a life driven by purpose.

For more information, visit: www.derrickserianni.com

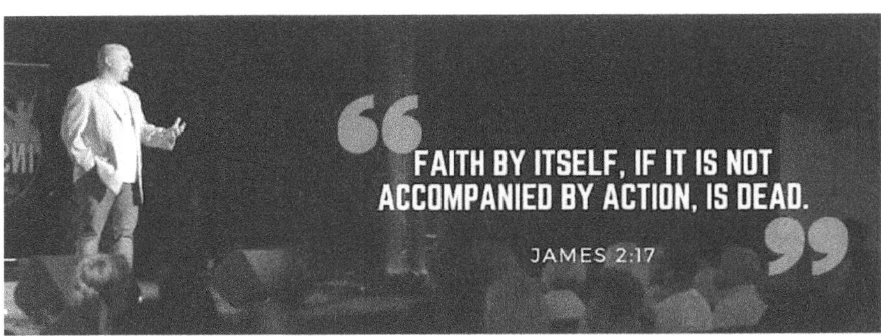

www.ingramcontent.com/pod-product-compliance
Lightning Source LLC
Chambersburg PA
CBHW040750120726
48005CB00012B/1126